WONDERS OF THE WORLD

# ST. LAWRENCE
## RIVER AND SEAWAY

**Terri Willis**

Technical Consultants

**John B. Adams III**
Senior Staff Engineer
St. Lawrence Seaway Development Corporation

**Captain Jim Perkins**
Marine Officer
St. Lawrence Seaway Authority

*Austin, Texas*

**A production of B&B Publishing, Inc.**

**Editor** – Jean B. Black
**Photo Editor** – Margie Benson
**Computer Specialist** – Dave Conant
**Interior Design** – Scott Davis

**Raintree Steck-Vaughn Publishing Staff**

**Project Editor** – Helene Resky
**Project Manager** – Joyce Spicer

**LIBRARY OF CONGRESS CATALOGING-IN-PUBLICATION DATA**

Willis, Terri
St. Lawrence river and seaway / Terri Willis
p. cm. -- (Wonders of the world)
Includes bibliographical references (p.) and index.
ISBN 0-8114-6370-2
1. Saint Lawrence River -- Juvenile literature. 2. Saint Lawrence Seaway -- Juvenile literature. [1. Saint Lawrence River.] I. Title. II. Title: Saint Lawrence river and seaway. III. Series.
F1050.W52 1995 94-3023
971.4--dc20 CIP
AC

Cover photo
**Cargo boat on St. Lawrence Seaway near Cap-a-l'Aigle, Québec**

Title page photo
**Montréal, Canada, on the St. Lawrence River**

Table of Contents page photo
**Ship in Iroquois Lock, St. Lawrence Seaway**

## PHOTO SOURCES

Cover Photo: © Valan Photo

ANQ, Québec, P600-5/GC-18: 20
Canadian Coast Guard, Laurentian Region: 22, 48, 53, 54 top
Canadian Wildlife Service/Québec Region: 49 bottom
Canards Illimités Canada: 11, 52
Photo Courtesy of Eastman Kodak Company: 61
Industry, Science, and Technology Canada Photo: 1, 4, 10 top, 46, 54 bottom, 56 top
New Bedford Whaling Museum: 16
New York State Department of Environmental Conservation/Wildlife Pathology Unit: 47
Ontario Hydro: 5, 31, 32, 34 bottom, 35, 38 bottom
Parks Canada: 55
Parks Canada/J. Beardsell: 12 bottom, 13, 56 bottom, 60
Parks Canada/Brian Morin: 3, 7 , 9, 10 bottom, 12 top, 18, 21, 45, 50, 57
Power Authority of the State of New York: 14, 15, 39
Robert Queen: 59
Photo Courtesy of Reynolds Metals Company: 44
© Eugene Schulz: 27
The St. Lawrence Seaway Authority: 23
St. Lawrence Seaway Development Corporation: 7, 20, 29, 33, 34 top, 38 top, 40, 41, 42, 43
Thousand Islands Land Trust: 49 top
U.S. Department of Transportation/Maritime Office: 28
U.S. Fish and Wildlife Service Photo by Craig Koppie: 58 top
U.S. Fish and Wildlife Service Photo by J.P. Mattson: 58 bottom
US Fish and Wildlife Service Photo: 13, 51 top
Wisconsin Department of Natural Resources: 17, 51 bottom

Printed and bound in the United States of America.
1 2 3 4 5 6 7 8 9 10 99 98 97 96 95 94

# Table of Contents

# Chapter One

# River of Destiny

The boom of the gigantic explosion sent shock waves for miles. Thirty tons of dynamite ripped open the huge temporary dam that had been built to hold back the waters of the mighty St. Lawrence River during the construction of the power plant on the river.

The power plant would produce electricity using energy supplied by the flow of the water. It would also provide power for an enormous engineering project—the St. Lawrence Seaway. The seaway would also tame sections of the St. Lawrence River that flowed through the provinces of Québec and Ontario in Canada and along New York State's northern border. In places, swift currents and fierce rapids had previously made travel on the river difficult and dangerous.

Now, large modern ships could sail the St. Lawrence from its mouth at the Atlantic Ocean all the way to the Great Lakes ports in Canada and the United States. The seaway would open the door to greater trade with Europe and the world.

On that July morning in 1958, the exploding dynamite unleashed the waters that had been held back by the dam. The flow was channeled to create a new lake, Lake St. Lawrence, which would provide the water supply needed by the power plant.

*"The statesmen made a treaty. . . . They would tame the River to men's uses.*

*"Did the River hear the faint scratching of the pens? Was the sound of cameras perceptible beside the fall of Niagara, in the whirlpools, eddies and rapids? No, the River only smiled that morning and went about its spring business of breaking the winter's ice, for it knew men would never tame it."*

**— Bruce Hutchinson, in *The Unknown Country***

**Early morning fog and mists hang over islands of the St. Lawrence River *(left)*.**

**Gaping holes were blasted in this 600-foot (183-m) temporary dam on July 1, 1958. Water ripped away the rest of the dam, as it rushed to form Lake St. Lawrence, the reservoir for the seaway's major power plant.**

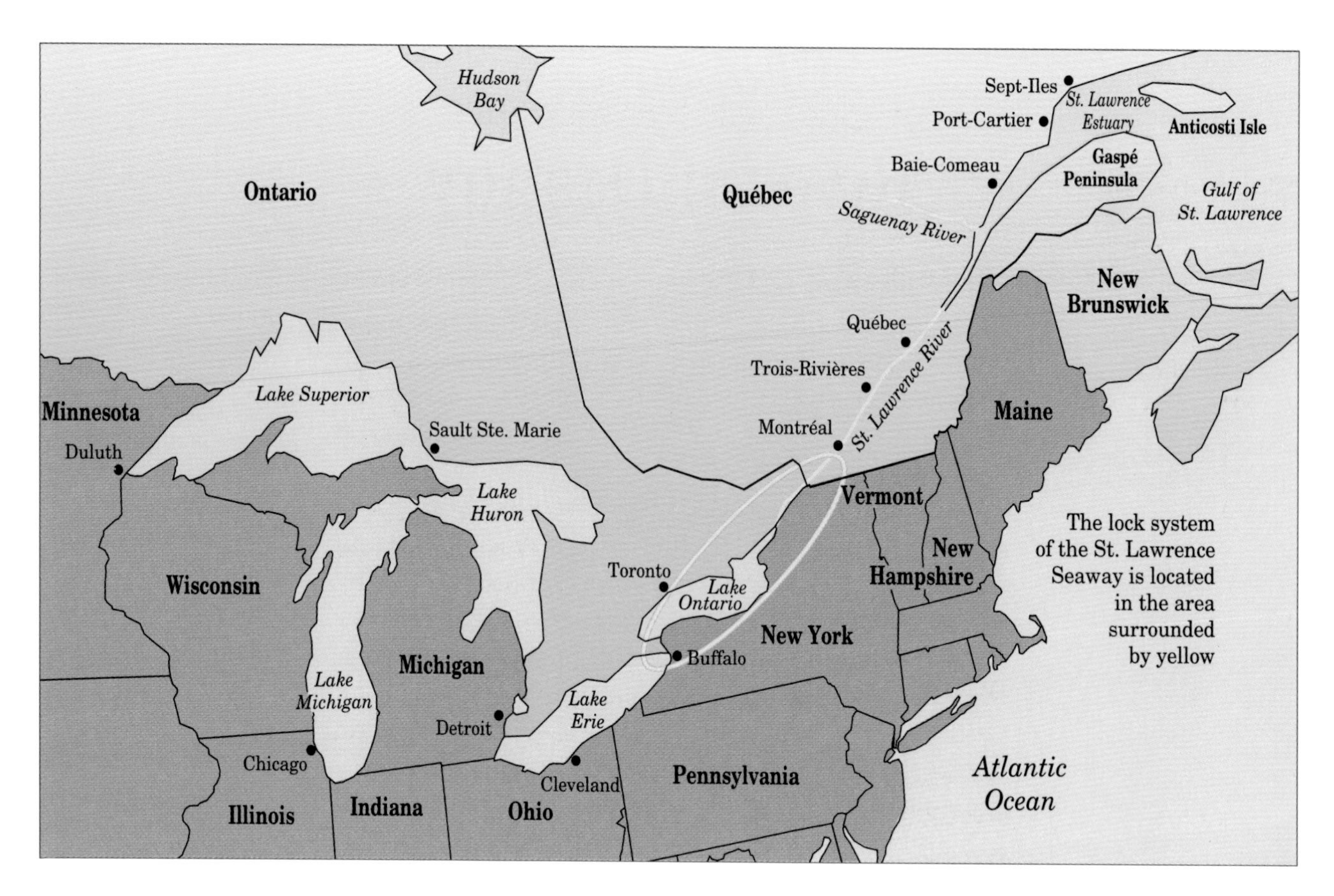


**The Great Lakes St. Lawrence Seaway System stretches all the way from Anticosti Isle in the Gulf of St. Lawrence to Duluth, Minnesota. The lock system of the seaway is located in the area surrounded by yellow.**

This lake covered land that once grew corn and beans, held homes, supported villages, and provided jobs for the people.

As the water flooded into its new boundaries, it covered over the past—trees, plants, animals, roads, churches—in a rush toward the future—a future of international business trade, industry, and energy. Some people lost part of their history, while others looked forward to better times.

The process of building the seaway continued. In that process, the St. Lawrence River was changed forever.

## River and Seaway

The mouth of the St. Lawrence River is located in the Canadian province of Québec on the Gulf of St. Lawrence. Looking more like a broad arm of the gulf than a river, it begins to narrow as it parallels the border separating Canada and the United States, only about 30 miles (48 km) away.

The river links the two major Canadian cities of Québec Province, Trois Rivières ("Three Rivers"), and Montréal. Then it goes on to Cornwall, Kingston and Lake Ontario, the source of its waters. But Lake Ontario is just the first of the Great Lakes.

The seaway is both larger and smaller than the

## NAMES FOR THE WATERWAY

- St. Lawrence River — the natural waterway from the Gulf of St. Lawrence to Lake Ontario.
- St. Lawrence Seaway — the man-made series of connecting channels, lakes, and locks that extends 346 miles (557 km) from Montréal to Lake Erie; the circled area on the map.
- St. Lawrence Seaway System — the 2,342 miles (3,769 km) of canals, rivers, lakes, locks, and public and private ports that extend from the Gulf of St. Lawrence at the Atlantic Ocean, along the St. Lawrence River, and through the Great Lakes, to Duluth-Superior on Lake Superior. Sometimes called the Great Lakes-St. Lawrence Seaway System.

river. It is a bit difficult to define because different organizations use different terms to describe it. We will use the terms, shown above, used by the St. Lawrence Seaway Development Corporation.

In this book, we will look closely at the St. Lawrence River and at the seaway structures and their effect on the river. But it is impossible to discuss the seaway without also considering the entire seaway system, for it is all linked in the unending flow of water to the sea.

Throughout history, the St. Lawrence River has affected humans. Perhaps no other river played so large a part in the early history of the settlement of North America. But humans have affected the river, too. To understand its challenges—present and future—we must first understand its past.

A laker navigating through the Dwight D. Eisenhower Lock where a ship traffic control center is also located

# Chapter Two

# Exploring the River

*"The blue of the St. Lawrence is not a blue of the sea or the sky, it is a blue of earth, a terrestrial mystery, one in being with those huge shores and the great earth stream, a blue of the lower atmosphere floating over the dark green of North America. Changing in terms of light, paling or darkening with day and hour, it is fundamentally one mood of color, one dusk of blue gathering a whole continental region into its composure and austerity."*

**— Henry Beston, in *The St. Lawrence***

Ice was the first ruler of this land. Great, massive sheets of ice called glaciers ground across the land that we now know as the St. Lawrence region. They determined where the valleys would lie and where the hills would rise.

The Ice Age glaciers that covered much of the northern half of North America carved out a huge depression in the region. When the ice slowly melted about 12,000 years ago, that depression filled with water, forming what came to be called the Chamberlain Sea. Over the next several thousand years, the land continued to shift, and the floor of the sea was lifted upward, causing the water to drain out. As the waters flowed northeastward to the Atlantic Ocean, they carved out the channel we know as the St. Lawrence River.

The glaciers also hollowed out the five basins that, together, hold the largest concentration of fresh water on Earth—the Great Lakes. Today, these huge lakes drain into the Atlantic through the St. Lawrence River system. The water moves 2,342 miles (3,769 km) from the Minnesota city of Duluth on Lake Superior to the Atlantic Ocean.

## Following the Water

The river system begins in chilly Lake Superior, which accumulates large amounts of water from the rivers of Ontario, Minnesota, Wisconsin, and Michigan. Superior, the largest of the Great Lakes, can be calm at times in the summer months. However, autumn gales cause the water to churn furiously. Waves toss high into the air, often putting ships in danger.

The moving water passes between the Upper Peninsula of Michigan and Ontario at Sault Sainte Marie. As it heads southeastward through Lake Huron, it enters a slightly warmer climate. Again the water passes down a river—the St. Clair—and into Lake St. Clair before rolling past Detroit. But then the water again heads northeastward in Lake Erie and rushes over the mighty falls of the

**Today, pleasure craft ply the beautiful waters of the St. Lawrence River where early explorers once sailed deep into the heart of the continent *(right)*.**

V
25
2283
ALBANY N.Y.

The sight of ships along the St. Lawrence Seaway is a fact of everyday life for the millions of Canadians and Americans that live by the water.

Niagara River into Lake Ontario, where it finally forms the St. Lawrence River. On the water's northern journey to the river's mouth at the Atlantic Ocean, the weather grows colder, ending in a semiarctic climate at the Gulf of St. Lawrence.

During its journey, the water takes on moods as varied as the climates. In some places, such as the Thousand Islands region, the flow is calm and constant. In this 40-mile (64-km) section, Lake Ontario empties into the St. Lawrence River. Here, the water flows amid more than 1,700 islands. Some are little more than rocky bumps in the water, bearing a tree or two. On other islands there are several homes, even elegant mansions.

In other sections of the river, the waters take a wild ride over breathtaking rapids. The entire river system drops more than 600 feet (180 m) in elevation along its course. Sometimes the descent is in short drops over rapids. Other times it is in large, spectacular falls—particularly the 167-foot (51-m) drop of Niagara Falls, on the Niagara River between Lakes Erie and Ontario.

Plunging 167 feet (51 m), Niagara Falls was the largest natural barrier to water travel along the St. Lawrence before the Welland Canal was built.

The St. Lawrence, which is about 11,000 years old, is a relatively young river compared to most on the planet. And it's not even particularly long—three river systems in Canada and seven in the United States are longer. Nevertheless, the area in which the St. Lawrence River meets the Atlantic Ocean is truly unique. The estuary of the river (the broad waterway where the river's fresh water meets the ocean's salt water) is the largest in the world. The huge area where salt and fresh water mix contains a rich assortment of nutrients to sustain an incredible array of wildlife.

Today, the St. Lawrence is still a working river. It supports a very healthy shipbuilding industry. Its mighty current produces electricity for cities. It helps bring raw materials to steel mills and smelting plants. It is used by pulp barges to carry logs from Forestville, Québec, to Québec City, and ships on the St. Lawrence carry goods between major North American ports and exotic places around the world.

For the past 150 years, the St. Lawrence has been a vital passageway. Immigrants used it to reach the interior of the North American continent. The river's fertile shores supported livestock and agriculture, and its moving waters powered mills that ground grain into flour.

A century before that, the St. Lawrence River was a vital trade route for fur trappers and explorers. And even earlier, Native Americans relied on it to travel throughout the region.

## Plants and Animals

For thousands of years after the glaciers melted and before humans arrived, the region was almost a paradise. Forests of spruce, maple, elm, oak, birch, and hemlock graced its shores, providing homes for many animals. Elk, moose, and deer grazed on the tender grasses and fed on roots and berries that

As many as 500,000 snow geese flock to the wetlands along the St. Lawrence River during their spring and fall migratory journeys.

A great blue heron near Lac Saint-Pierre in Québec

grew along the river. Bears, wolves, and foxes preyed on many of the smaller animals that made their homes there, such as martens, beavers, rabbits, raccoons, squirrels, muskrats, skunks, and opossums.

Overhead flew great flocks of waterfowl. The river provided an excellent habitat for these birds. Geese, ducks, loons, and gulls built their nests on the river's banks. Twice each year, large flocks of white snow geese used the river as a stopping place on their seasonal migration. In late spring and again in autumn, they landed near the Gulf of St. Lawrence and fed for several weeks on tender roots before they continued on their journey.

The river waters were home to millions of fish. Lake trout up to 5 feet long (1.5 m), huge whitefish, record-sized muskellunge, and pike, as well as smelts, bass and perch made the river a fisherman's paradise.

## The Magical Saguenay

In a region now called the Saguenay Fjord, the Saguenay River from the north pours into the narrowing estuary of the St. Lawrence River. Here, where the St. Lawrence is very deep and nearly 20 miles (32.2 km) wide, salt from the ocean mixes with its waters. Together, the two rivers create a unique habitat for many animals of unusual varieties.

Fresh surface water flowing from the Saguenay lies over a deeper, very cold layer of salt water from the Gulf of St. Lawrence. This mix produces water that is low in temperature, high in oxygen, and rich in nutrients. Plankton and other small plants and animals, such as crustaceans, thrive in such waters.

The large amount of plankton in the waters of Saguenay Fjord attracts its most remarkable feature—the concentration of whale species unlike anywhere else on Earth. The mouth of the Saguenay River is the only place where four whale species—belugas, or white whales, minke, fin, and blue whales—are found in such a small area.

A St. Lawrence beluga whale in Saguenay Marine Park

Walruses, too, once flourished in the shallow waters, along with other marine creatures. The St. Lawrence River had an enormous array of wildlife—until European settlers came.

Created in 1990, Canada's Saguenay Marine Park, located where the St. Lawrence and Saguenay rivers meet, protects the remaining St. Lawrence beluga whales.

## A New Inhabitant

Life along the St. Lawrence remained unchanged until humans arrived in the area. The first people to reach the land surrounding the Great Lakes and the St. Lawrence River came from the north about 10,000 years ago. Their early ancestors had probably come from Asia by way of the Aleutian Islands, which extend southwest from what is now Alaska. As generations came and went, the people continued to move eastward, gradually reaching the St. Lawrence region, where they later became known as Algonquin Indians.

The Algonquins were skilled at living off the land. They were good hunters and knew where to find the best wild fruits and vegetables. They were also good craftsworkers, building solid homes of bent saplings covered with birch bark. Their sturdy canoes, also made of the bark, were the first boats to sail on the Great Lakes and the St. Lawrence River.

The second migration of Native Americans came from the south centuries later. Over many generations, the new people, who would later be called Iroquois, traveled northward to the St. Lawrence region, probably from the Gulf Coast.

These newcomers were interested in politics and government. Each of their villages had a large "longhouse," made of saplings and bark, which was used as a meeting place for warriors and chiefs. But homes and other buildings in their villages were rather shabby and carelessly built. They were interested in

Known for their love of warfare, the Iroquois pushed the Algonquins west out of the St. Lawrence area in the early 1600s. Protected by the French, the Algonquins later returned, resettling in Ontario and Québec.

social things and were far less skilled than the Algonquins were at such crafts as building. The Iroquois boats, for example, were simply hollowed-out logs.

The tribes into which the two main groups of Native Americans split often fought each other, but those who lived in the St. Lawrence Lowlands did little harm to the natural wildlife of the area. Although they hunted and fished—and some even mined copper—the environment recovered from what they did to it.

## Enter the First European Explorer

The next migration of humans came long afterward when Europeans began to be curious about the continent. Many historians say that the first Europeans to arrive in the region were Norsemen about A.D. 1000. Known as Vikings, they sailed in small boats from Iceland to Greenland, and on down the coast of North America, traveling past the mouth of the St. Lawrence. But the Norsemen did not stay long.

The real exploration of the continent started after Christopher Columbus arrived at the Bahama Islands off North America in 1492. He did not get near the continent itself, but other explorers soon came. British, French, and Dutch explorers were early visitors to North America. Most were mainly interested in finding an easy water route across North America—a "northwest passage" to shorten their travel time to the Orient. However, others, excited by the thought of a "New World," explored its shore and eventually reached the mouth of the St. Lawrence River.

*The "People of the Longhouses" envied the well-crafted boats of the Algonquins and the warm furs they wore in the winter. What they wanted, these people took by force, and thus began centuries of vicious fighting between the Algonquins and these longhouse Indians, who came to be known as the Iroquois, which means "the Destroyers."*

Frenchman Jacques Cartier was one such explorer. In 1534 he persuaded his king, Francis I, to finance a journey to find a northwest passage through North America. Failing to find it on his first try, he set sail again in 1535. On August 10 of that year, he discovered a 100-mile- (161-km-) wide gulf that led to a great river. Because August 10 was the feast day of St. Lawrence, Cartier named the gulf in the saint's honor. The river he named the "River of

Canada." About a hundred years later, the river took on the same name as the gulf.

*"Along both shores, we had sight of the finest and most beautiful land it is possible to see, being as level as a pond and covered with the most magnificent trees in the world."*

**— Jacques Cartier in his journal**

Cartier and his men solicited the help of some friendly Algonquins to act as guides on a journey up the river. With his men, Cartier sailed up the wide river to a spot where it narrowed, becoming deep and swift. He called the spot *Kebec*, an Algonquin word meaning "narrows." The area later became known to the French as Québec.

The large sailing vessels Cartier commanded could not proceed farther up the narrow river. Cartier hoped to send two Algonquins ahead to explore, but they refused, fearing battles with the Iroquois, who lived there. Cartier and a few of his men went instead.

They traveled about 120 miles (193 km) to the site of a series of treacherous rapids near what is now Montréal. Cartier named them *Sault La Chine,* which means the "rapids of China," because travelers seeking a passage to China through Canada would first

**In 1534 French explorer Jacques Cartier was welcomed by the St. Lawrence Iroquois. When Cartier later captured some Iroquois chiefs and carried them off to France, he turned their original welcome into enduring hostility.**

need to find a way past these rapids (now called the Lachine Rapids). Cartier could not get past. He returned to Québec.

The French stayed through the winter, but many died from disease and the bitter cold. Before leaving in the spring, Cartier claimed the land for France. Cartier learned on his return home that he was considered a failure because he had not found a northwest passage.

Nearly 70 years later, in 1603, a French navigator and cartographer named Samuel de Champlain was selected by the king of France, Henry of Navarre, to go to the New World. Like Cartier, he was to seek a northwest passage, but he had additional tasks—to convert the Native Americans to the Roman Catholic religion and to bring furs to France.

Although he had earlier failed to establish a colony at the Bay of Fundy, in 1608 Champlain was put in charge of 32 colonists who were to officially found the French colony of Québec. During the first winter, Champlain and his crew began a trip up the St. Lawrence River in smaller boats than Cartier had used. By portaging (carrying their boats), they made it around the Sault La Chine. They traveled across two lakes that are formed by the river and

The St. Lawrence attracted not only trappers who built a prosperous fur trade but also seamen ready to slaughter walruses and whales for profit.

on to another large rapids (now called International Rapids) in the area now bordered by New York.

Champlain and his men returned many times over the next three decades to explore more of the St. Lawrence River and the region surrounding it, which they called New France. They mapped much of the area, became fast friends with the Algonquins, and took many fine furs back to the markets of France—markets that would soon demand more and more fur from the New World. Champlain is sometimes called the "Father of Canada" for his success in opening the land to more people.

## A Trade Route Develops

By the mid-1600s, the nature of the region began to change. It was still wild, inhabited mostly by Native Americans, but Europeans were coming to the land in great numbers. They were drawn by the expanding fur trade. Pelts from animals such as beavers, otters, and moose, which lived along the St. Lawrence River, became all the rage in Europe, and their value soared.

The St. Lawrence River became a busy trade route where French trappers and natives alike traded highly-prized beaver pelts for supplies at many settlements along the waterway.

As canoes and boats laden with furs sailed down the river toward ships bound for Europe, the St. Lawrence River became a popular trade route. At many posts along the way, trappers could trade their furs for various supplies before heading out into the wilderness again. The French trappers were called *coureurs de bois*, or "runners of the woods." Assisted by the Algonquins, they controlled the fur trade.

The English and the Dutch, meanwhile, were also interested in furs. Because the French controlled the area north of the river, the English and Dutch formed trading alliances with the Iroquois, who provided them with lesser quality furs taken from animals living farther south. (Because of the warmer climate, animals that lived south of the river didn't need to grow such thick coats each winter as those north of the river did.) The Iroquois soon head-

A red fox of the St. Lawrence region, one of the animals hunted for its fur

ed north across the river on raids to get better furs.

Over the years, tensions between the Native American nations became worse as they struggled over who had rights to the land. The French and English fought, too, over who controlled important forts, trading posts, and even developing towns. As the battles became more ferocious, the French joined forces with the Algonquins, while the English and the Iroquois became allies.

The French and Indian War, fought from 1754 to 1763, is also known as the Seven Years' War. Both the French and the British won some battles and lost others, but the turning point for the British came when they took Montréal from the French in 1760. France's last grasp on Canada was gone. The war ended in 1763 with the signing of the Treaty of Paris, which granted most North American land to the British.

The fur trade on the St. Lawrence River slowed for a time, as the French abandoned their trading posts. But eventually, other Europeans took over. The river grew busier than ever before.

New immigrants came to the area, particularly from the British Isles. These people were interested not so much in furs as in settling the land and farming the fertile soils of the region. But before they could begin, they faced a major obstacle—trees! Tall trees, strong and wide, grew thick and plentiful throughout the area. Each one had to be cut down and the stump removed by hand before a new farmer could even begin to work the land.

While many people hated the trees they had to cut down, others began to see profits in the timber harvest. They quickly built sawmills along the St. Lawrence River in places where there was enough movement in the river to provide power. Logs were floated down the river and its tributaries. The lumber was in great demand for shipbuilding, for construction in the other British colonies, and for export to the West Indies.

## ONTARIO'S FIRST WOMAN "DOCTOR"

Ontario's first woman "doctor" hailed from the little town of Dickinson's Landing along the St. Lawrence River, one of the oldest villages in Canada. Granny Hooples was a young girl when the rest of her family was killed by a tribe in the area, and she was kidnapped. She lived with the tribe for seven years before she was released, and during that time, she learned many of the Native American ways of using roots and herbs to treat various illnesses and injuries. Returning to the European settlement, Granny Hooples successfully used these methods on local residents for many years in the early nineteenth century and was greatly loved for her skill.

Lumber camps became big business throughout a large part of Canada. The men in the camps tore up the land, hunted for food, cut down the trees, and then failed to replant where they cut them down. The St. Lawrence River became a main transportation route for the timber, as well as for furs, wheat, and other products.

## The Land Without Cities

Most young men in the St. Lawrence region grew up expecting to earn a living working on the river, and few received any formal schooling. The general lack of education helped slow urban growth along the river.

Although Québec existed before any city now in the United States except St. Augustine, Florida, it was mainly a military fort. Montréal was a trading post. Most other cities along the St. Lawrence have similar histories of developing for one reason. But while the United States may have had a more successful urban start, the St. Lawrence River gave Canada an edge in international trade.

Trees growing along the St. Lawrence River include white pine and white oak.

White Pine

White Oak

With its waters navigable from the Atlantic Ocean all the way to Montréal, the St. Lawrence enabled much of Canada to maintain easy trading ties with many European capitals. In these fashion-craving centers of civilization, the demand for Canadian furs was strong. And as the trappers and traders sought to expand into the wilderness to meet the demand, the development of urban centers was neglected. Expansion into the countryside was too important.

Beavers do not like to live near people and their developments. They like to live out in the wilderness, where the waters are clear and undisturbed. When beavers build their dams along streams, they create ponds that eventually become filled up with silt, turning into smooth green meadows. These changes that they make in the wilderness have long played a major role in creating a habitat for many animals.

The trade in beaver furs, the country's major business in the eighteenth century, followed the animal to the remote corners of the St. Lawrence region. The lumber trade, too, gradually moved out into the wilderness.

Urban centers were not necessary—or even desirable —for people living along the St. Lawrence River. Therefore, very few cities developed. The people could continue to prosper as long as nothing happened in the shipping industry to make the river less important. But with so many valuable natural resources, more and more settlers came, bringing new ideas for growth and change.

**Québec's harbor was a bustling place in 1759. But very few other urban areas had developed at that time.**

# Chapter Three

# The Seaway Takes Shape

The St. Lawrence River region was becoming an economic hub of North America. Ports in Montréal and Québec were especially busy, but the increasing river traffic helped draw attention to one big problem—the river's rapids. Rivers always run downhill, from the source to the mouth, usually in a smooth and gentle incline. A rapids, however, is a section of a river where the riverbed rock is so hard that it has not been eroded and smoothed by the water. Instead, the water rushes over rough rock like an elongated waterfall.

Loads of furs and timber could be moved much more quickly and efficiently on the St. Lawrence if the turbulent waters didn't pose such a threat. And there was a solution—canals, man-made waterways that rerouted the river through a smooth channel, thus bypassing the rough spots.

## Early Canals

Actually, a canal around the Lachine Rapids had been attempted just as the St. Lawrence was becoming a trade route. In 1680, Dollier de Casson, an energetic young French priest, began planning a mile-long canal to bypass the Lachine Rapids section. It took several years to get his enormous project under construction. And when work finally began, the changes he and his men made in the river angered the Iroquois, who revered the natural majesty of the St. Lawrence. In 1689, the Iroquois attacked, murdering 200 French settlers.

Enthusiasm for the canal dwindled, and in 1701, de Casson died and the money ran out. Only about 2,000 yards (1,820 m) of the canal had been carved out of the rock. The trench remained, and the river continued to reign in its natural glory for nearly 75 more years.

The British and Canadians built Fort Wellington at the end of the St. Lawrence Rapids during 1838-39. Any supplies going to Toronto or cities farther upriver had to pass by the fort. The fort has been restored for visitors.

The American Revolution, which began in 1776, spurred the English again to think about building a canal. They realized that troops would be slowed down if they had to navigate around the rapids.

A series of small canals was built to bypass not only the Lachine Rapids, but several smaller areas of rapids and falls as well. However, these shallow canals were satisfactory to travelers for only a short time. People were changing the kind of boats they used on the river from canoes and small rafts to larger boats. The larger craft had keels underneath to steady them and therefore required deeper water.

**Lighthouses warn of shallow places in the river.**

Sometimes large barges and paddlewheel ships, often piloted by river-wise captains, bypassed the small canals on their way down the river. They "shot the rapids" instead, giving their passengers a memory for life.

*"Everybody crowds toward the bows, to watch the big ship plunge down the boiling flood. We can see the great breakers heaving and tossing . . . and in one moment more we are on the Rapids.*

*"What shall I say of the sensation? My wife, who is a venturesome body, was disappointed. She wanted a bigger fall, a more sensational leap, and a greater chance of getting her neck broken. But . . . I found the waves quite big enough and fierce enough to make my heart jump a little against my watch-pocket, and my breath catch again in my throat at each respiration."*

**— A passenger on a boat shooting the rapids**

## Overcoming Obstacles

In the end it was business that caused the second wave of canal building along the St. Lawrence. Easy navigation was necessary for Canadian goods to travel to the ocean, where they could be traded on the international market. The young country to the south, the United States, was cutting into the Canadian trade market and planned to build a spectacular canal that would link Lake Erie to the Hudson River, which flows into the Atlantic. In order to keep up, Canada had to make the St. Lawrence more navigable. Work began immediately, and in 1825, the same year that the Erie Canal was finished, a new Lachine Canal also opened to traffic.

Four years later, an even greater obstacle farther inland was overcome. Niagara Falls between Lakes Ontario and Erie was not just a simple rapids. Instead, there was a 326-foot (99-m) difference in elevation between Lakes Erie and Ontario. Most of it comes at the 167-foot (51-m) drop at Niagara Falls. No riverboat captain, even the most foolhardy, was going to try to "shoot" that!

But William Hamilton Merritt had another solution. He sold people on the idea of a 9-mile- (14.5-km-) long canal to bypass Niagara Falls in a series of 40 locks—a sort of stairway—far fewer than would be used later. Merritt ran out of money working the hard rock, but a Canadian who recognized the importance of the canal stepped in and completed it. The first Welland Canal was opened for business in 1829.

When the original Welland Canal opened on November 30, 1829, Lake Erie and Lake Ontario were joined and Niagara Falls was bypassed. The canal required a series of 40 locks to raise and lower the boats.

## Never-ending Changes

Sailing vessels could now go from the Atlantic Ocean all the way to Lakes Huron and Michigan. But then another dangerous rapids at Sault Sainte Marie blocked their passage into Lake Superior. The Soo Canal was built there in 1856, and for the first time, ocean vessels could make their way into all the Great Lakes.

The canals carried boats needing a water depth of up to 9 feet (2.7 m). But almost as soon as the Soo Canal was finished, new, larger ships requiring 14 feet (4.3 m) began to replace the old ones. By 1867, all the canals had been deepened to allow these larger ships to go through. But by then, even larger ships were on the horizon.

It became clear that to remain an international shipping lane, the St. Lawrence route would have to be dug to a depth of 20 feet (6 m). The expense would be huge, and the project would require cooperation between Canada and the United States. Many people wondered if two nations could ever work together on such a major project.

There were a few options. The United States could plan such a deep route on its own, along the path of the Erie Canal. Canada could reroute part of the St. Lawrence, keeping all within its boundaries and deepening it. Or the two nations could cooperate to make an efficient seaway that would be accessible to large ships.

The final option was the most efficient and least costly, but at the turn of the century, it didn't seem very likely to happen. A gigantic international seaway project had never before been undertaken.

## The Slow Pace of Politics

The main problem was politics. It was easy to see that working together to improve the seaway would benefit both countries. But before that could happen, politicians in both countries would have to make compromises, and that rarely happens easily.

For one thing, the opening of the Erie Canal had caused some hard feelings in Canada. For the first time, trade from Canada and the United States as well was diverted away from the St. Lawrence River and into the United States. From that time on, most improvements in water transportation came as a result of competition between the United States and Canada. Each nation did what was needed to make its transport routes the most successful.

Newspaper cartoons such as this one showed that not all Canadians were in favor of a seaway project.

Each continued to make improvements to the St. Lawrence system in its own territory, deepening a canal here, widening a lock there. The seaway was not stagnant, locked in a time warp, but neither was there an organized effort to bring it up to the needs of the twentieth century and beyond. From time to time, one or the other of the two countries seemed prepared to reach an agreement, but something else always got in the way.

Some people felt that the demand for a deep waterway was obvious—that such a waterway would pay for itself quickly and help the economies of both countries. Others disagreed, saying that the need was unproved, that the new seaway would be extremely expensive, and that better railroads could

# HOW LOCKS WORK

Locks raise and lower ships by putting water and the law of gravity to work. They don't need pumps to operate.

The basic structure of a lock is an enclosed area called the chamber, made with concrete walls, watertight gates at each end, and valves that admit or release water. A ship going upstream (toward the river's source and to a higher elevation) enters the chamber through the downstream gate, which closes behind it. By opening valves at the upper end of the filling tunnel, water flows from the lock above to the lock below through openings located along the bottom of the lock walls. The rising water lifts the ship until the water level is the same on both sides of the upstream gate. The gate opens and the ship leaves the chamber.

When a ship is going downstream, it sails into the chamber, and the gate is closed behind it. Valves at the lower end of the filling tunnel are opened, and water flows out. The ship slowly descends with the water level, until it can sail out the downstream side.

Each process uses more than 22 million gallons (83 million l) of water, but it takes only about 10 minutes to raise or lower a ship. Complete passage through a single lock takes about 30-45 minutes, since the ship must maneuver in and out slowly.

## THE WELLAND CANAL

The oldest section of the seaway, the Welland Canal, connects Lake Ontario with Lake Erie. Built by Canada, the first canal opened in 1829 to bypass Niagara Falls. It was only 8 feet (2.4 m) deep and required a 40-lock "staircase" to lift ships the 326 feet (99 m) to meet Lake Erie's waters.

Rebuilt three times, today's Welland Canal begins at Port Weller on Lake Ontario and extends 26 miles (42 km) to Port Colborne on Lake Erie. It is now 27 feet (8 m) deep and has eight locks. Seven of these locks are located near the northern end of the canal, with three of them connected one after another like three giant stairs similar to this drawing. The eighth lock, called a guard or control lock, is located at the southern end of the canal and is very shallow. This lock guides ships into Lake Erie. It takes approximately eight hours to navigate through the canal.

To ensure safe and timely passage through this link of the seaway, Canada completed a seven-year rehabilitation program during the winter of 1992-93. The work cost approximately $175 million.

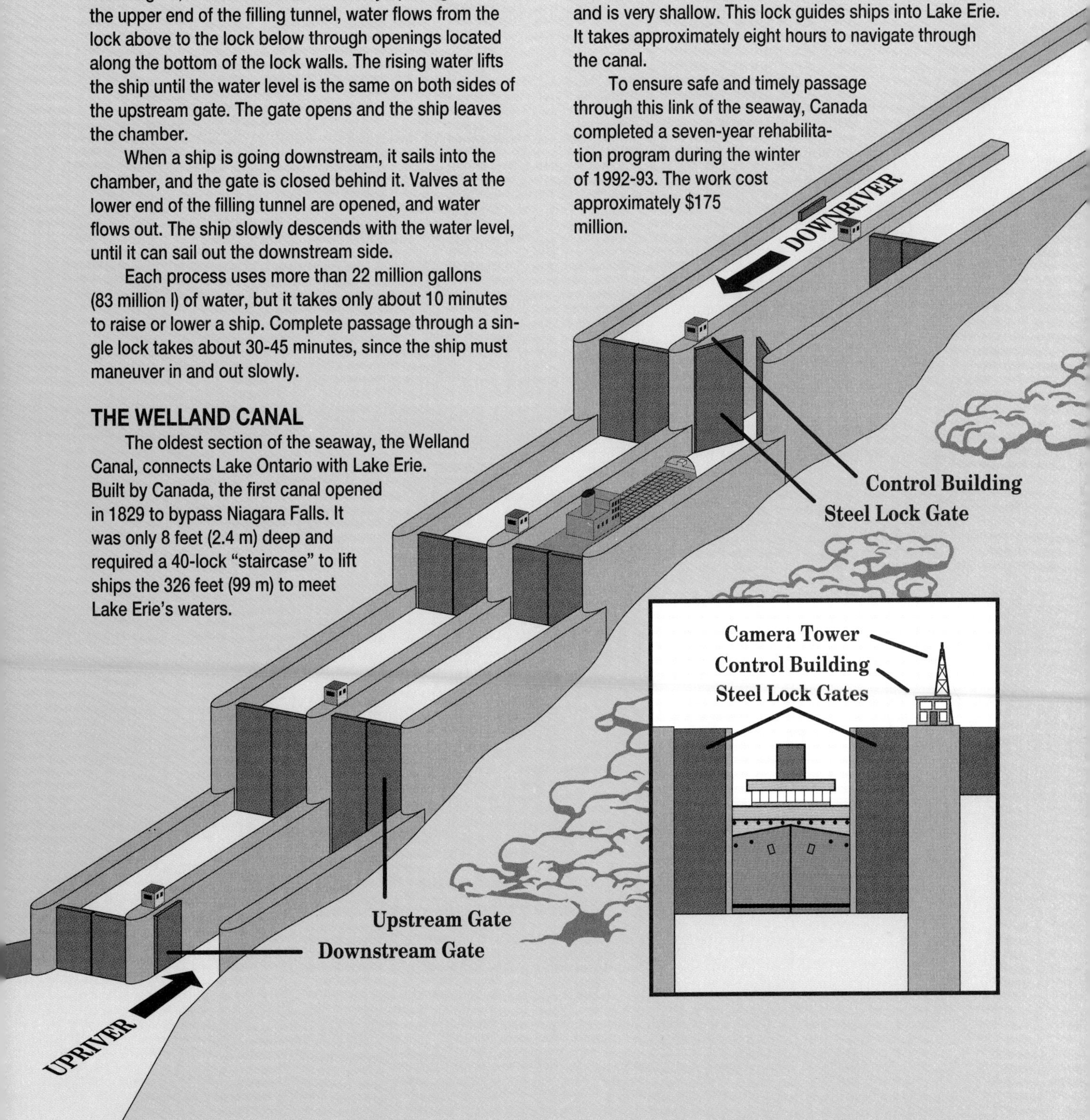

## THOUSAND ISLAND DRESSING

While the controversy surrounding the international seaway project dragged on, something else was happening along the St. Lawrence River that also caught international attention: the creation of Thousand Island dressing!

This popular salad dressing is a mixture of mayonnaise, catsup, and pickle relish. It was created in the early 1900s by Sophia LaLonde, who lived in Clayton, New York, along the Thousand Islands section of the river, shown at the left. Clayton was a popular resort area, and LaLonde's husband, George LaLonde, Jr., guided visiting fishing parties on the St. Lawrence. He enjoyed treating them to his wife's unusual dressing during shore dinners at the end of the day.

One visitor, Mae Irwin, a prominent New York City stage actress, was particularly impressed with the dressing and gave it its name. She took the recipe to the owner of New York's famous Waldorf-Astoria Hotel, where it was immediately put on the menu. Thousand Island dressing quickly became a favorite around the world.

handle the growing demand for transport.

Some said that both water and rail transportation systems were necessary to boost the economy. Others argued that while taxpayers in both countries would share the burden of the cost to improve the St. Lawrence, only a few would benefit.

Over the decades, most heads of state in both countries, including U.S. presidents of the time, were in favor of the seaway. However, strong anti-seaway lobbies in both countries prevented agreements.

In 1941, the two countries finally entered a pact to construct power and navigation facilities on the St. Lawrence. However, before legal questions could be settled, World War II got in the way. Once again, the project was dropped.

Not everyone wanted the idea to die, however. Canada, in particular, began a strong push for seaway improvements after the war. The idea of doing the work on their own started to gain favor with many Canadians as U.S. delays mounted. President Harry Truman, a supporter of a joint waterway, worked hard to get the United States involved. In the spring of 1952, Truman sent letters to the U.S. Senate and House of Representatives calling for the United States to join Canada's effort. Still, no action was taken.

*"The question before the Congress now is not whether the seaway should be built, but whether the United States should share in its construction, operation, and control. The Canadian Government is ready and willing to build a deep seaway from Montréal to Lake Erie on the Canadian side of the boundary, if Congress does not authorize the United States government to participate in building the joint Canadian-United States Seaway agreed to in 1941."*

**— President Truman, 1952**

## Life Goes On

In the meantime, as the controversy droned on, the people who lived along the St. Lawrence River went on with their lives, confident that the seaway was not going to interfere. They built homes and cottages, played in treehouses, and shared first kisses on the riverbanks. They worshiped in the churches along the shores and buried their dead in nearby cemeteries. Most lives were not extraordinary, but filled with the everyday memories that eventually made it heart-wrenching to leave.

And that's exactly what happened when Canada and the United States finally settled on an agreement. Most people had gone on with their lives, thinking that a compromise would probably never be reached and that they wouldn't have to worry about it. But when the two countries reached agreement at last, it meant the beginning of great changes in the lives of many people.

Agreement was reached in 1954. The Canadian Parliament became fed up with years of fruitless negotiations. "The biggest and longest dragging of feet I have known in my entire career is that of the Americans on the St. Lawrence," stated Lester Pear-

The seaway promised growth for such cities as Montréal. However, the picturesque towns of the Gaspé Peninsula, shown here, maintain the flavor of an earlier time and a slower pace.

A major reason for building the seaway was to accommodate large ships loaded with grain, iron, and other products, from the Great Lakes region.

son, Canada's secretary of state for external affairs. Giving up, the Canadians finally decided to manage the project on their own. There would be an all-Canadian waterway, complete with power plant. It was time to move.

Such a decision was a hard blow for the U.S. government! If Canada went ahead on its own, then the United States could be the big loser. It would lose both an important trade route and rights to the massive amount of electricity that could be generated.

The U.S. government sent out a frantic message: "Wait for us! We're coming along!" And they did.

*"Rivers, together with mountains and deserts, have been long considered as natural barriers which make excellent national frontiers because they divide peoples from one another . . . [But] More and more, this great waterway has become a bond rather than a barrier between Americans and Canadians."*

**— Louis St. Laurent, long-time Canadian supporter of a joint seaway project, 1954**

## Agreement Is Reached

The Wiley-Dondero Act, which called for American participation, was passed by Congress in 1954. The two countries then signed an agreement that began work on the St. Lawrence Seaway—work that would make it a major North American trade route, one of the finest in the world!

The St. Lawrence Seaway from Montréal to

Lake Erie would include canals that were deepened to 27 feet (8 m). Construction workers would dig through dry land, as well as dredge the river bottom to make the route safe for most of the world's large ships. There would be a series of locks and dams that, taken together, would lift ships about 600 feet (183 m) above sea level as they moved 2,000 miles (3,219 km) inland.

In addition, a massive power plant along the river would provide energy to the seaway, as well as to parts of Canada and the United States. Construction of the seaway and its management would be the joint responsibility of the St. Lawrence Seaway Authority in Canada and the American St. Lawrence Seaway Development Corporation.

## Getting Out of the Way

The haggling between governments was finally over. But it was only the beginning of haggling for thousands who lived along the river.

The major cause of problems for the residents was the hydroelectric power plant to be built along the Long Sault Rapids, in the International Rapids section of the river. It was one of the seaway's main selling points. Not only would it produce enough electricity to power locks and dams on the seaway, but the extra electricity could also be used for power in Ontario and much of New England in the United States.

Such a power plant required the building of a dam that would create a huge water reservoir more than 30 miles long and up to 4 miles wide (48 by 6.4 km). This artificial lake, to be called Lake St. Lawrence, would flood 18,000 acres (7,285 ha) in New York,

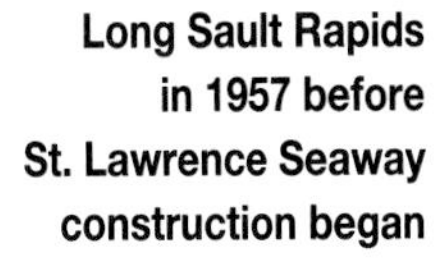

**Long Sault Rapids in 1957 before St. Lawrence Seaway construction began**

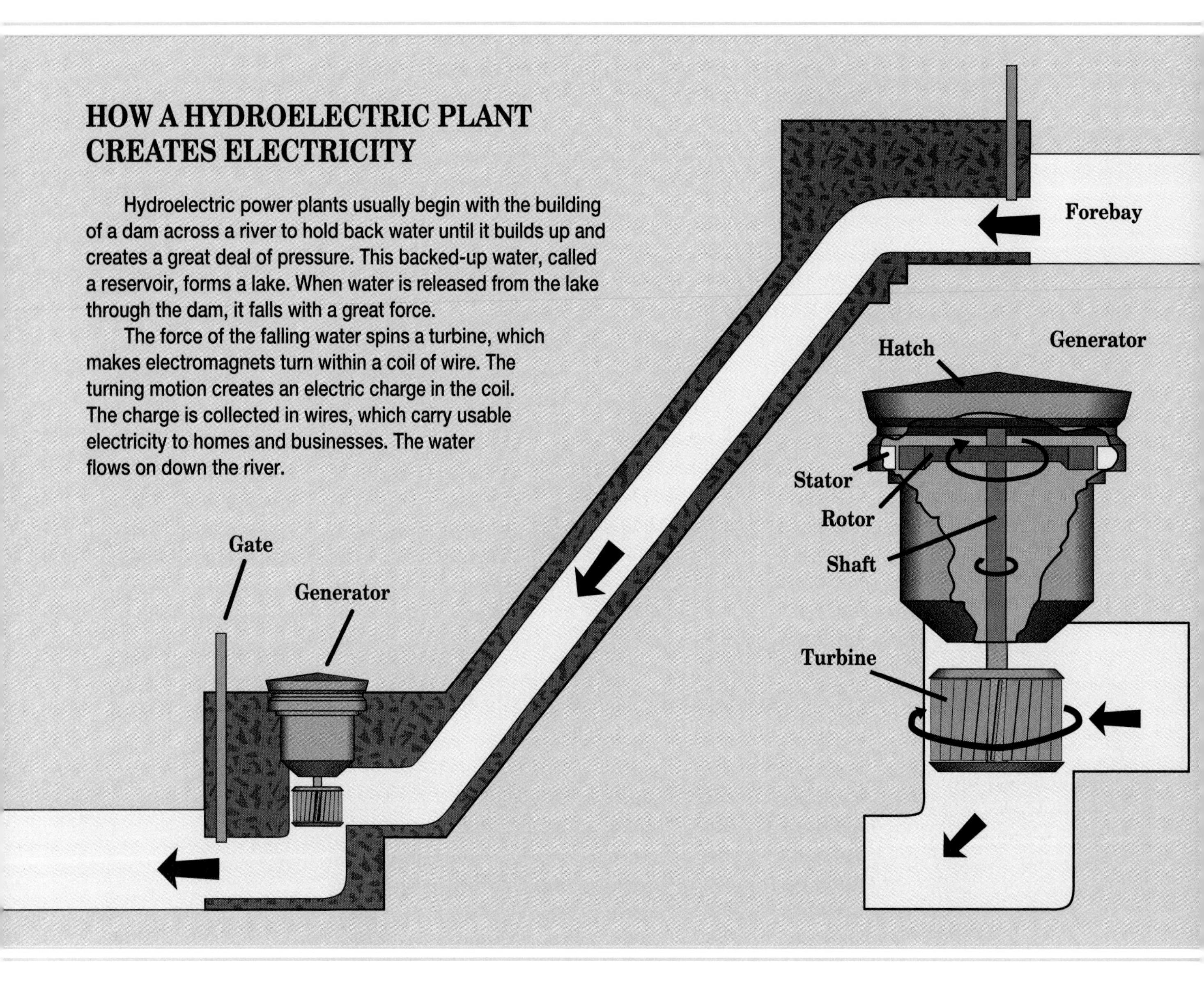


covering land that held more than 600 homes and 200 farms. In Ontario and Québec on the Canadian side, 20,000 acres (8,094 ha), including 3 towns, 4 villages, more than 200 farms, 40 miles (64 km) of railroad, and 35 miles (56 km) of highway, would be flooded. All told, more than 8,000 people had to be moved. Little thought was given to the many animals that would lose their homes.

Moving people off their land, some seaway engineers later said, was their biggest headache. Governments had the right to seize the land, but they were required to make fair payments to owners. Just what was fair payment became the question.

One engineer, after a day of haggling over payment, made the following remark. "My next canal will be dug across a desert, a thousand miles from the nearest human habitation."

The costs of moving people were to be shared

equally by the Hydro-Electric Power Commission of Ontario, known as Ontario Hydro, and the New York Power Authority. These agencies would control the power plant.

Some farmers barred surveyors from their fields, while others ordered bulldozers off their land. Some refused to leave their homes, saying they would stay until the water flowed through their front door, carrying them away. One elderly woman kept agents away from her home with an old gun.

Some of those who refused to move eventually received much larger amounts of money from the agencies than did people who had cooperated. When news of this got around, more people tried to stay on their land and fight, looking for big money. Finally, the agencies got tough. On a Caughnawaga Indian Reservation, one woman who had refused to move was hanging out laundry in her yard one morning when a bulldozer smashed down her home.

*Owners of homes being moved were instructed to leave possessions, even fine china, in their places, and were guaranteed that nothing would be damaged. They were told to leave a full glass of water on each kitchen table. After the houses were moved, they could judge whether the homes' contents had been upset by how much water was spilled.*

## Moving the Masses

Moving whole towns was another matter. In 1955, the town of Iroquois, Ontario, was the first to be displaced. As the time approached, many people took on a hopeful attitude. "We have to go, but watch us grow," became an unofficial motto.

Representatives of Ontario Hydro visited every affected family, business, school, and church. They offered to construct new homes or buildings, or to move the old buildings onto new concrete foundations. They also promised to make any construction repairs necessary, paint the houses, and complete the landscaping.

Existing homes were moved by two huge machines built in New Jersey at a cost of about $100,000 each. The machines were not like anything else in the

**One of the 525 houses moved from the old town of Iroquois to the new site, 1.5 miles (2.4 km) north**

The village of Iroquois, Ontario, once stood on the flooded area near the river's shore. The Iroquois Control Dam and the new Iroquois Lock made relocation of the entire town necessary.

world. With tires about 10 feet (3 m) high and arms large enough to reach around a whole house, they could move the entire building without upsetting anything inside.

After the houses had been moved, their owners' favorite shrubs followed. And if the owners wanted their homes placed next door to their old neighbors, that, too, was arranged.

While many people chose new homes, others chose to keep their old homes, which gave the newly transplanted communities a more stable atmosphere. All residents received new foundations, new plumbing, and new wiring for their homes, along with new streets, industrial parks, shopping centers, and schools. But for many people, new amenities could not replace the excitement of living along the river, watching the ships pass by, and feeling a part of the flow of the water.

Even years later, those who had lost their homes would sometimes take out boats and look down into the water. They remembered the joys and the sorrows they had experienced and shared, down below Lake St. Lawrence.

# Chapter Four

# Engineering Spectacular

*"I know of nothing that should so appeal to the imagination of the people of North America as the final consummation of the struggle of generations to open these Great Lakes as a part of the Seven Seas."*

**—U.S. President Herbert Hoover, in 1927, long before the seaway was completed**

As the canals were dug and the dams were built, the new St. Lawrence Seaway began to take shape. It was the largest construction project ever carried out jointly by the United States and Canada, so it attracted a lot of attention.

Every day, especially on weekends and pleasant evenings, throngs of people would gather along the St. Lawrence shoreline to watch the enormous drills, shovels, and trucks reshape the land. The fascinated viewers crowded onto nearby observation towers provided by the Seaway Authority. The men at work below looked like swarms of busy ants. As many as 22,000 men worked on the project at any given time.

Without question, the task was awesome. The precise engineering required for the project was a massive undertaking. Never before had such a powerful river been rearranged in such a major way. The thousands of homes and hundreds of towns that lined its banks would be in serious danger if a mistake caused the river to flood. An error in the water level of only 3 inches (7.6 cm) could spell disaster—too high, and villages would become

**Engineers designed the Long Sault Dam to curve gracefully from the mainland of New York to the tip of Barnhart Island where Long Sault Rapids once churned.**

islands; too low, and ships would be grounded.

In the end, none of these potential problems ever occurred. The seaway project was completed successfully within its four-year deadline, becoming the most ambitious and effective alteration to the face of the Earth that people had ever undertaken.

## Construction

The huge concrete interior walls of the Dwight D. Eisenhower Lock under construction

Construction of the seaway itself began in September 1954. The total estimated cost was about $1.2 billion, with more than half that amount going to the power plant alone, which had been started a month earlier.

That's a lot of money today, and at that time, it was a staggering sum! But think about the work this project required. Just the amount of soil that needed to be moved is mind-boggling—more than 210,515,000 cubic yards (160,950,000 cu m). This much earth could fill Chicago's Sears Tower—the world's tallest building—more than 90 times! If that amount of soil were put into railway cars, the line would reach across North America eight times!

Excavating all that land proved challenging. Builders encountered rock, clay, and other geological formations that were much more difficult to deal with than had been anticipated. The rock, glacial till (compacted earth that resembles rock), and heavy clay of the region were incredibly tough. Dealing with these materials became one of the construction teams' largest problems. Shovel teeth and bulldozer blades that lasted a year under normal working conditions wore out in a few days—sometimes in a matter of hours. Drills that could usually bore through 50 or 60 feet (15 or 18 m) of rock before wearing out

Bulldozers and graders moved and leveled tons of earth for the new seaway, sometimes threatening or damaging the beautiful French architecture of many old buildings in Canada.

## ST. LAWRENCE SEAWAY PROFILE

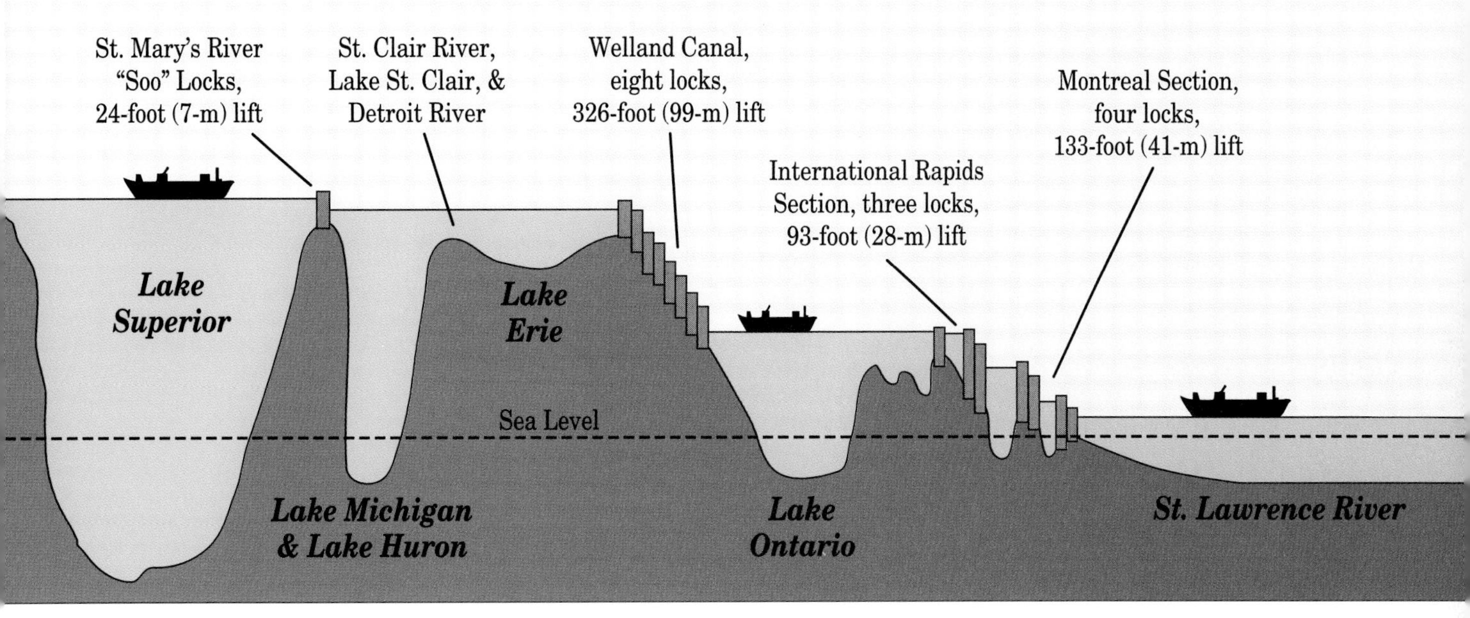


went bad after 5 feet (1.5 m). These equipment problems naturally drove costs higher.

Another major task was increasing the depth of the river by dredging. Large machines called draglines pulled enough soil and muck from sections of the river bottom to make sure it was at least 27 feet (8 m) deep. Most of this work was completed in the American portion. In particular, a stretch of the river from Ogdensburg eastward to the Eisenhower Lock required deepening.

Bridges over the river presented another challenge to seaway engineers. New seaway specifications required that bridges be high enough to allow ships up to 120 feet (37 m) tall to pass under them, but in many cases, this was not possible. Each bridge presented its own individual problems. Some bridges had lift spans installed, sections that could be raised when a tall ship needed to pass under it. At others, however, the road traffic was so heavy that any sort of lift that would interrupt the flow of traffic would result in huge traffic jams. These bridges had to be raised, sometimes by as much as 50 feet (15 m). Four bridges in the city of Montréal alone had to be raised.

The U.S. share of the seaway project included the digging of the Wiley-Dondero ship channel to bypass the power dam at Barnhart Island (the dam that would later be called the Moses-Saunders Dam). Canada constructed three separate canals and five locks to bypass dams and areas of rapids. The

**The seaway improvement project was carried out in several different locations. Work was done along the Welland Canal between Lakes Erie and Ontario, as well as at several spots along a 190-mile (306-km) stretch of the St. Lawrence River, from the Thousand Islands region to Montréal.**

## ROUTE OF THE ST. LAWRENCE SEAWAY

Ships traveling upriver begin their St. Lawrence Seaway journey out in the Gulf of St. Lawrence, almost 1,000 miles (1,609 km) from Montréal. At Les Escoumins, north of the mouth of the Saguenay River, commercial ships take on professional pilots who guide the vessels through the river's narrowing channel, dangerous curves, and shallow waters. This portion of the river must be dredged regularly. Fog, wind, and heavy traffic add to the navigational hazards. Hundreds of buoys, lighthouses, and other aids mark the safe route. Most of these aids are concentrated between Grondines, Québec and Cornwall, Ontario.

Before entering the lock and canal system near Montréal, each ship owner must obtain permission to use the seaway. When safety and financial regulations have been met, a vessel is given an identification number and allowed to move on. Vessels traveling on the seaway must stay in upbound or downbound shipping lanes to minimize the possibility of collisions.

From Montréal to Lake Ontario ships pass through seven locks. A large light panel is located at the end of each lock. By watching these lights carefully, a ship's pilot can time the arrival of his vessel so as to avoid costly delays. For example, a non-flashing green light means the lock is ready, a series of yellow lights indicates the amount of time left before a ship can enter the lock, and a flashing red light means there is more than one ship in the lock.

The first four locks on the seaway are Canadian. St. Lambert Lock and Côte Ste. Catherine Lock are located across the river from Montréal, Québec. Sixteen miles (25.7 km) to the west, ships pass through the Lower and Upper Beauharnois locks. The next two locks—the only ones administered by the United States—are located 60 miles (97 km) upriver near Massena, New York. The first, Bertrand H. Snell Lock, is separated from the Dwight D. Eisenhower Lock by 3 miles (4.8 km) of the Wiley-Dondero Canal. The last lock in this 190-mile (306-km) portion of the river is Iroquois Lock, located at Iroquois, Ontario. The next 80 miles (129 km) to Lake Ontario is marked by the beautiful scenery of the Thousand Islands region.

Power-generating dams and control dams occur along the portion of the river where the lock system is located. The Moses-Saunders Power Dam, built during seaway construction, produces electricity. The Beauharnois Power Dam was built earlier. Various control dams, such as the Long Sault Dam, regulate the level and flow of water to ensure proper water depth for ships.

Ships travel 180 miles (290 km) across Lake Ontario before reaching the Welland Canal. With eight separate locks, the canal lifts ships 326 feet (99 m) to meet Lake Erie's waters. This is the biggest lift along the entire seaway. To avoid delays, these locks have been "twinned" (built side by side) to allow two-way traffic. There are no locks past the Welland Canal unless vessels are bound for ports on Lake Superior, and then only one lock must be passed at Sault Ste. Marie.

Pleasure craft are also welcome on the seaway, but they have to meet certain size requirements. A boat must weigh a minimum of 1,984 pounds (900 kg) or be at least 20 feet (6.1 m) in length. Commercial craft are always given preference in the lock system, however.

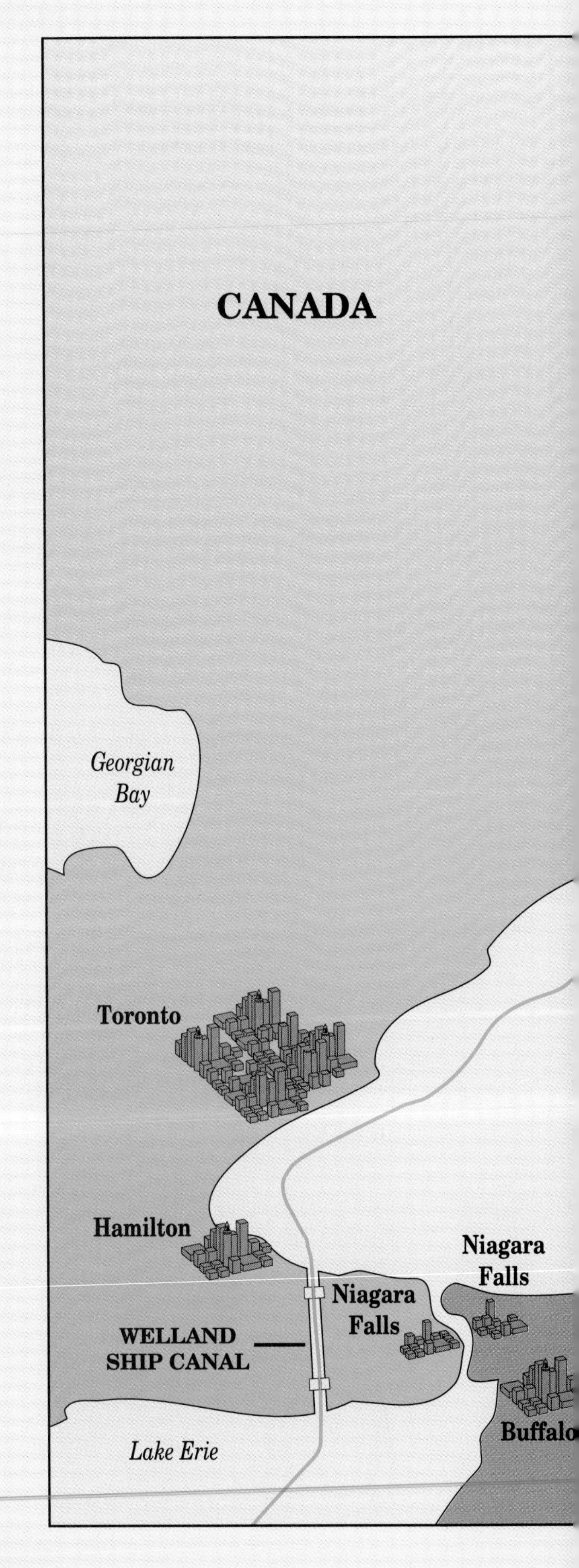

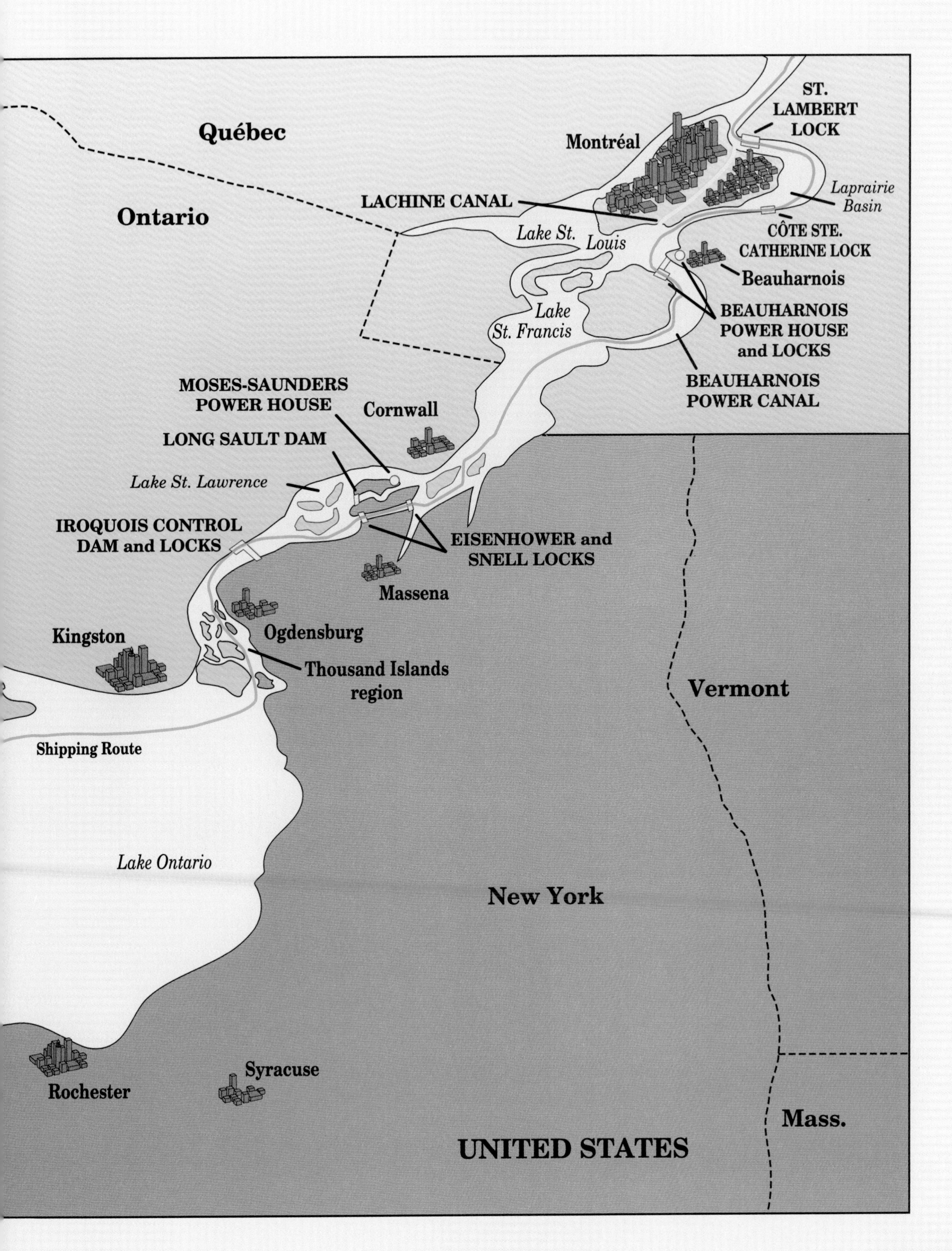
Québec
Ontario
Montréal
ST. LAMBERT LOCK
LACHINE CANAL
Laprairie Basin
Lake St. Louis
CÔTE STE. CATHERINE LOCK
Beauharnois
Lake St. Francis
BEAUHARNOIS POWER HOUSE and LOCKS
BEAUHARNOIS POWER CANAL
MOSES-SAUNDERS POWER HOUSE
Cornwall
LONG SAULT DAM
Lake St. Lawrence
IROQUOIS CONTROL DAM and LOCKS
EISENHOWER and SNELL LOCKS
Massena
Kingston
Ogdensburg
Thousand Islands region
Vermont
Shipping Route
Lake Ontario
New York
Rochester
Syracuse
Mass.
UNITED STATES

A series of canals, locks, and dams was carefully designed by seaway engineers. All the locks, including the Dwight D. Eisenhower Lock, were built to handle ships as long as 730 feet (223 m) and no more than 76 feet (23 m) wide. All canals were dug to a depth of 27 feet (8 m) to match the existing depth of the Welland Canal.

Canadians also deepened the Welland Ship Canal to 27 feet (8 m) in 1932. The locks on the St. Lawrence River were built to the same size as the locks already existing on the Welland Canal. A 70-mile (113-km) section near Montréal was also dredged.

Most of the canals built were lined by dikes (canal walls) constructed from materials removed from the land along the way. The glacial till was an excellent building material, creating sturdy dikes.

One of three water intake portals of the Moses-Saunders Power Dam during construction

## Building the Power Plant

Building the hydroelectric power plant at the International Rapids section brought special challenges. A series of dams was installed clear across the river at the head of the rapids to transfer water to a giant excavated cut. As the waterflow down the rapids decreased, the huge boulders that had made the rapids so treacherous were exposed inch by inch, and soon the river bed was dry.

Construction workers could then begin work on one of the major sections of the seaway, extending from Cornwall, Ontario, up the river about 50 miles (80 km), to Prescott, Ontario, near the end of the Thousand Islands region. This particular section, one of the most beautiful parts of the river, contained many small islands and raging rapids.

Workers changed the gradual drop across the International Rapids to a steep drop at a single point. At this point, where 110 million gallons (416 million l) per minute plunge 85 feet (26 m), the water of the St. Lawrence provides energy necessary to create electricity.

Water enters the dam through grated openings to drive 32 turbine-generator units. The 32 generators produce 2,200,000 horsepower of electricity (1,880,000 kilowatt hours or 1,600,000 kilowatts of power).

The power plant itself is actually one building 3,300 feet (1,006 m) long, but the imaginary line of the International Boundary passes through it, so it is considered to be two buildings. Each "building" contains 16 generators.

The original power plant was called the Barnhart Island Powerhouse, but later each nation's half was renamed. The Canadian section is the Robert H. Saunders–St. Lawrence Generating Station. Saunders worked for many years on the power project. The American half is the Robert Moses Power Dam, for the chairman of the Power Authority of New York.

**The Moses-Saunders Power Dam was the largest structure built during seaway construction. Half of the dam belongs to New York State and the other half to the Canadian province of Ontario.**

When the Moses-Saunders Power Dam was finished, it was the second largest power plant in North America—only Washington State's Grand Coulee Dam was slightly larger—and it was the only power plant built, maintained, and shared by two nations. Now, there are close to 50 larger dams, and several are joint projects.

In New York, industries located near the power source use much of the electricity produced. In Ontario, people and businesses located in the southeastern portion of Ontario are the major buyers of power.

U.S. President Dwight D. Eisenhower and Britain's Queen Elizabeth II were two powerful political forces supporting the St. Lawrence Seaway project.

## The Seaway Opens

Finally, the work on the seaway was completed. There had been many problems, but workers finished the enormous task on time.

On July 3, 1958, about 100 ships that had waited both in the Great Lakes and in the St. Lawrence River began churning through the locks. The shorelines of the Great Lakes were officially classified by Congress as the fourth U.S. coastline.

It was another year before the seaway officially opened. On June 26, 1959, Queen Elizabeth II came from England for the celebration. The royal yacht *Brittania,* banners flying, sailed up the St. Lawrence, with U.S. President Dwight D. Eisenhower on board.

The completion of the seaway, said the President, "is a tribute to those farsighted and persevering people who across the years pushed forward to their goal despite decades of disappointments and setbacks."

"It is a magnificent monument," said the Queen, "to the enduring friendship of our two nations."

During the first year, the St. Lawrence Seaway carried about 20 million tons of cargo. However, traffic jams were caused by slow-moving ships whose captains were unfamiliar with the seaway. Some ports on the Great Lakes were not prepared to handle the large number of vessels that arrived. Sometimes ships had to wait several days to be loaded and unloaded.

A few of the problems faced in the first year were temporary, but others linger. The St. Lawrence Seaway has brought with it many successes, and difficulties, too.

# Chapter Five

# Success and Failure

The first grand ship down the new St. Lawrence Seaway carried the Queen of England and the President of the United States. Later cargoes were not so glamorous. But then, that depends on how things are viewed.

People whose incomes depend upon the Seaway System may likely consider a mountain of wheat to be rather attractive. That's because wheat is the main commodity transported on the seaway—12 million tons of it were shipped in 1991. Iron ore was next, with 7 million tons.

The other major commodities transported on the seaway include different grains and coal, as well as manufactured steel and iron products. Through the years, the St. Lawrence Seaway has transported more than 1.1 billion tons of cargo, worth more than $200 billion.

*"At the end of a century marked by fabulous progress in science and technology, we are taking a new step forward in our collective awareness concerning the state of the environment.*

*"We have put an end to the uncontrolled exploitation of our natural resources. And we want to stop the thoughtless dumping of toxic substances into our natural environment. In short, we have arrived at a moment of truth—a sense of individual and collective responsibility which will lead to a viable future, in economic as well as ecological terms."*

**— Lucien Bouchard, Canada's Minister of the Environment, 1988**

## Economic Effects

Moving all that cargo has helped to move the local economy along, too. A 1993 report shows that the Great Lakes Seaway System has created a total of 44,628 jobs in the United States. Most of the jobs are on ships and in ports, while many more people work transporting goods to and from the ports. These jobs produce nearly $2 billion in income. The total income generated in Canada by the Seaway System is also estimated at about $2 billion.

**In order to keep the seaway from stopping development, highways had to go either over bridges or under the seaway itself. This ship is passing through the Dwight D. Eisenhower Lock, while cars can go underneath.**

Iron ore in the form of taconite pellets accounts for one-third of all seaway cargoes. The ore is hauled from Canada's mines to the St. Lawrence where it is shipped to steel mills located near Great Lakes ports.

In addition, the seaway has saved money for those who use it to ship their goods, since it is cheaper than other means of transportation. Certainly, the grains grown by the farmers of Canada and the United States must somehow first be transported overland to a port along the seaway. So, too, must the iron ore that comes from the Mesabi Range in northern Minnesota and the Québec-Labrador Range north of the St. Lawrence River. Usually these goods reach the port by train. But once loaded onto a ship on the seaway, these products will travel by one of the most efficient and least expensive means available.

Ships on the St. Lawrence Seaway System can move cargo from Chicago, for example, across the Atlantic to Europe for less than the cost of transporting the same cargo by train from Chicago to an eastern seaport on the Atlantic. This is an important savings in fuel, time, handling, and money.

*Seaway transport is energy efficient. A typical Great Lakes carrier moves about 1 ton of cargo 497 miles (800 km) on 1 gallon (3.8 l) of fuel. Trains could carry that cargo 199 miles (320 km) on 1 gallon of fuel; trucks, 60 miles (97 km); and aircraft, only 4 miles (6.4 km).*

All this shipping occurs during the approximately nine months each year that the seaway is normally open. Through the years, the opening day has been generally in late March or early April. It closes sometime between mid-December and early January because of ice.

It was obvious from the start that the seaway could be a tremendous boost to local economies. Overseas trade at the Great Lakes ports grew immediately and immensely in the year following the opening of the seaway. Increases of three to four times the previous year's trade were common. Kenosha, Wisconsin, for example, saw a 23-fold jump, and the Duluth-Superior port had a 78-fold increase. The greatest individual increase was in grain traffic. Chicago's overseas shipments of grain increased 21 times, and Duluth's, 110 times. The United States' new fourth seacoast had become the continent's chief grain-exporting coast.

One of the earliest problems following the opening of the seaway was the traffic jam of ships at the Welland Canal. At first, this problem had hardly been noticed by those who were excited by the business and industry the seaway would bring to their hometowns along the St. Lawrence River. Older than the rest, this section moved ships at a slower speed, and often, several vessels were backed up. In a six-year project completed in 1973, a new 8-mile (12.9-km) channel was built. It bypassed the city of Welland, Ontario, where slow drawbridges on the river had delayed ship traffic.

Lakers loaded with coal, coke, iron ore, petroleum goods, and grain are a common sight in the locks of the seaway.

## A Boon to Business

The new international shipping lanes and the increased amount of power available from the associated power plant helped attract Reynolds Metals to Massena, New York, located on the seaway. It employed about a thousand people, and it was the first major new industry to come into the Massena area in five decades.

The establishment of the Reynolds plant offered great hope to local residents and government officials alike, who saw it as a sign of economic growth. Reynolds joined Alcoa (Aluminum Company of America), which was also located at Massena. Alcoa was the largest producer of aluminum in the world, and Reynolds was the second largest. Shortly afterward, General Motors agreed to open a plant near the Reynolds factory to cast auto parts from Reynolds's aluminum. It would employ several hundred workers.

The Reynolds Aluminum Plant was built in Massena, New York, because the seaway was nearby.

Unfortunately, by the time the two new plants were opened, Alcoa had already automated several of its plant procedures. Machines now did jobs that once required workers, so the company cut its number of employees by about twice as many people as the new plants employed. So even with the new jobs, high unemployment continued.

Still, there was hope that the long-range benefits of the seaway's power, transportation, and recreational opportunities would help both New York's and Ontario's communities grow at a good pace. Québec had already seen new growth from the seaway by the time it was open. About $500 million worth of industry, particularly steel manufacturing, settled along the river near Montréal.

Overall, the profits and business growth resulting from the seaway's construction have been somewhat different for the United States and Canada. Because of the importance of the St. Lawrence River in Canadian history, any changes to the river had great impact on Canadians. In Canada, there are many natural resources, so transportation systems that allow these products to be carried long distances and traded with foreign countries are vital to its economic health.

While the United States also relies on the seaway, it has several more ports on the surrounding oceans than Canada has. In addition, there are other inland waterways that are used to transport goods. The Erie Canal, for example, leads toward the Atlantic. The Mississippi River, which empties into the Gulf of Mexico, is a major transportation route. But for people living in major U.S. cities along the seaway, the economic impact of the St. Lawrence Seaway is just as great as for those living in Canada.

## Added Benefits

The seaway has produced benefits other than economic ones, however. For example, when the seaway was built, some important roads and highways were lost or flooded. The agencies in charge rebuilt them elsewhere and often made them much better than the old roads.

In Ontario, major portions of Toronto-Montréal King's Highway 2—one of the most dangerous roads in the province—were flooded by the project. The 40 miles (64 km) that have been rebuilt are safe and attractive.

In New York, much of the river road between the towns of Waddington and Massena had to be replaced. Unlike most of the old roads in the region, which took drivers past junkyards and billboards, the new curving highway gives drivers views of lovely wooded areas and Lake St. Lawrence.

Canada's St. Lawrence Islands National Park lures vacationers to the river's beautiful island shores.

The Fort Prevel, Québec, golf course next to the St. Lawrence River offers recreation in a spectacular setting.

Parks were planned as part of the seaway project to make the area more attractive. In Ontario, six new parks were created along the river. In New York, a park established around the locks and dams near the power plant was later turned over to the state park system. Also, in many places along the seaway path, wildlife refuges were created, along with boat launches, golf courses, and scenic overlooks for travelers. Millions of trees were planted to cover the ground damaged by the construction.

The new trees and the parks that came with the seaway helped repair some of the damage caused by carving out the locks and canals. They also serve as homes for some of the animals that had been forced out of their habitats. Some of the natural beauty that was lost is beginning to be replaced.

## Hazardous Waste

But something more harmful than a loss of beauty was building up in the water that flowed past the parks. Little by little, silent and invisible, harmful chemicals made their way into the seaway system, causing serious pollution.

For one thing, there were many towns along the seaway on both sides of the border that had no sewage treatment systems. Raw sewage poured into the seaway untreated. Increasing numbers of ships were also dumping sewage into the water. Other sources of pollution were identified: local dumps and landfills leaked toxic chemicals into the water, and rain runoff from agricultural land carried fertilizers and pesticides into the water.

# TOXINS IN THE GREAT LAKES–ST. LAWRENCE SEAWAY SYSTEM

The region along the St. Lawrence has been a perfect place for industrial development, especially on the Canadian side. Various industrial operations—pulp and paper mills, petrochemicals, petroleum refining, metallurgy, explosives, textiles, and mining—discharge waste and toxins into the river, polluting the water and harming fish and other wildlife.

Before Canada implemented its St. Lawrence Action Plan in 1988, about 2.3 million pounds (1,043,300 kg) of harmful waste, from organic matter to oil, grease, and metals, were dumped into the river each day. And that didn't take into account urban and agricultural runoff.

Many toxins slowly settle out of the water and become part of the sludge—the mud and mire that line the river bottom. These contaminated sediments are found throughout the Seaway System. They would do little harm there if they just remained on the river bottom, but they don't. They are easily churned back up into the water by wave action and burrowing marine animals. They are also released through dredging—or scooping out the mud at the bottom of the river. This process poses another great challenge. Each year millions of cubic yards of sediment must be removed from the bottom of the Seaway System. Disposal of the sediment has become a major problem because various pollutants may have contaminated it as they settled out of the water. Usually the sediment has just been dumped in special diked disposal areas, but many of these areas are filling quickly, and sometimes the toxins seep through the soil into the groundwater below.

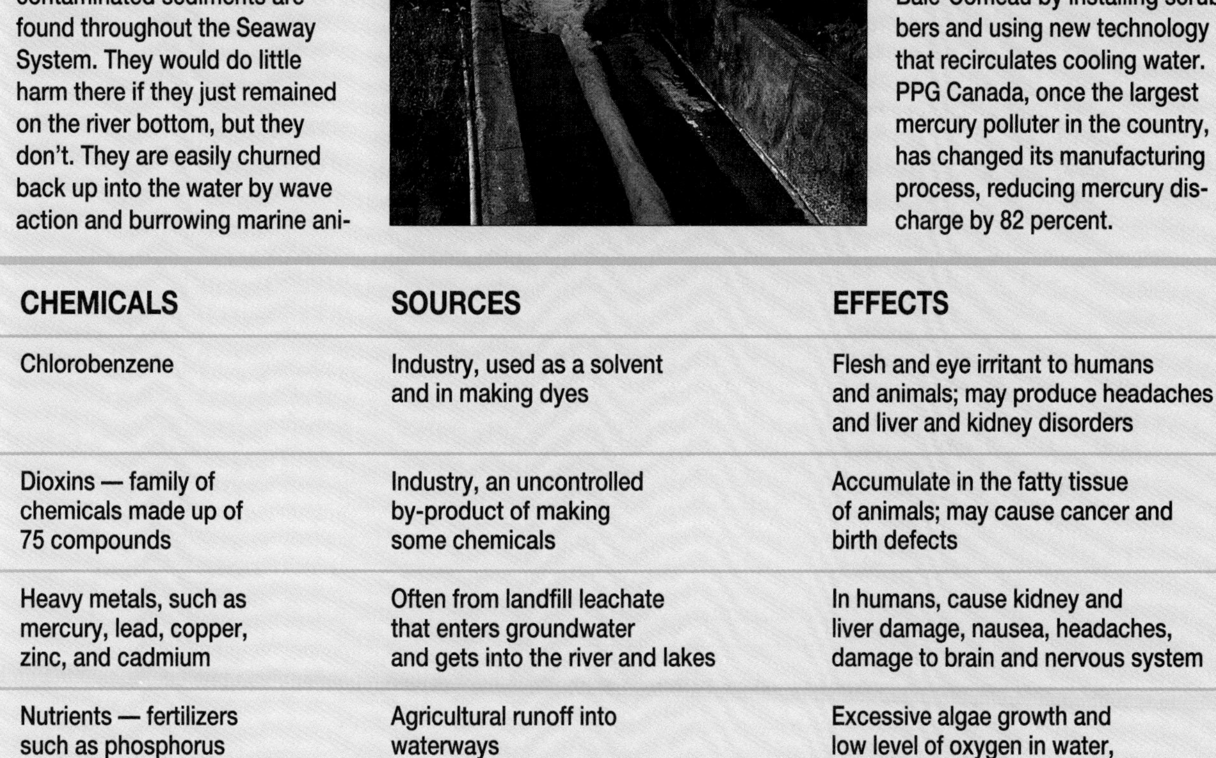

A better solution is needed. Many industries—forced by new regulations—are reducing their toxic discharge. For example, Reynolds Aluminum has almost eliminated its PAH discharge at Baie-Comeau by installing scrubbers and using new technology that recirculates cooling water. PPG Canada, once the largest mercury polluter in the country, has changed its manufacturing process, reducing mercury discharge by 82 percent.

| CHEMICALS | SOURCES | EFFECTS |
|---|---|---|
| Chlorobenzene | Industry, used as a solvent and in making dyes | Flesh and eye irritant to humans and animals; may produce headaches and liver and kidney disorders |
| Dioxins — family of chemicals made up of 75 compounds | Industry, an uncontrolled by-product of making some chemicals | Accumulate in the fatty tissue of animals; may cause cancer and birth defects |
| Heavy metals, such as mercury, lead, copper, zinc, and cadmium | Often from landfill leachate that enters groundwater and gets into the river and lakes | In humans, cause kidney and liver damage, nausea, headaches, damage to brain and nervous system |
| Nutrients — fertilizers such as phosphorus and nitrogen | Agricultural runoff into waterways | Excessive algae growth and low level of oxygen in water, limiting animal life |
| PAHs — Polycyclic aromatic hydrocarbons | Industrial waste, especially from coke production, petroleum refining, and trash incineration | May cause cancer in humans |
| PCBs — Polychlorinated biphenyls | From industrial sources, used in making many products; most enter water from air pollution | Skin damage, birth defects, liver damage |
| VOCs — Volatile organic compounds | From industrial sources | May cause cancer in humans |

The Canadian Coast Guard deploys pollution control equipment after an oil spill in the St. Lawrence River. Most oil spills on the river occur in ports.

Other poisonous materials enter the waterway from the ships. About 20 percent of all the goods transported on the Seaway System consists of hazardous materials such as petroleum. Spills of these chemicals can happen when there are many ships maneuvering on the seaway at close quarters to each other and to the port facilities. Even small spills of some chemicals can be very harmful to living things and the water supplies.

But the major cause of pollution in the river is the large number of industries located along the water. Reynolds Metals, for example, was dumping 6.4 million gallons (24.2 million l) of chemical discharge into the St. Lawrence each day. This toxic material contained not only PAHs, but also fluoride, aluminum, cyanide, and phenols.

Another company, Domtar Fine Papers from Cornwall, Ontario, was convicted in 1989 for excessive chlorine and chlorine dioxide emissions. The company paid a $12,500 fine.

## Wildlife and Pollution

The results of the pollution are many, and they affect the water quality of the whole Seaway System. The waters have become murky, while heavy plant growth on the river bottom outside the main shipping channel has made it too shallow for pleasure craft to pass easily. Chemicals collect in the bodies of fish, birds, and other wildlife, harming their health and making them unsafe to eat.

Cormorants are common waterfowl in the seaway

region. A study of cormorant embryos from Lake Michigan's Green Bay concluded that they had many more serious birth defects than were found in embryos collected elsewhere. The defects were probably caused by pollution in the water.

Throughout the seaway system, deformities have been found in wildlife because of toxins. Cormorants and other seabirds hatch with bills that cross, clubfeet, and missing body parts. Snapping turtles are found with open abdomens.

Of the ten most highly valued species of fish in Lake Ontario, seven have almost completely disappeared. In fact, toxic substances in the Great Lakes have had damaging effects on all fish populations. Salmon, trout, and whitefish do not reach full sexual development, and coho salmon and lake trout show enlarged thyroid glands.

Big sores show up on the bodies of other fish that were once healthy and plentiful in the St. Lawrence River. Some are deformed, and many have an unusual reddish cast to their gills.

Problems in fish can be harmful to the economy. Millions of people come each year to fish in the Great Lakes. Sport fishing on the lakes has an estimated value of $4 billion. Further destruction of fish populations could destroy this activity.

Swamps, bogs, fens, and marshes make up the wetlands of the Great Lakes and St. Lawrence River region. Wetlands are home to more than 220 species of birds, mammals, and amphibians. Fish depend on wetlands for their habitat, and migrating birds fly along them. Wetlands also protect against eroding shoreline and serve as a flood buffer.

**The common tern lays its eggs in river wetlands, which are threatened by pollution and development. Chemicals can seep through the eggshells, harming the young.**

## BIRD-CLEANING CENTERS IN QUEBEC

More than one million waterfowl stop along the St. Lawrence during fall and spring migrations, close to 500,000 breed in its wetlands, and 250,000 winter along its shores. Because oil-spill emergencies occur with some regularity along the river, its estuary, and gulf, six bird-cleaning centers have been established in Québec near areas with large concentrations of wildlife. Two other centers are planned for Mingan and Magdalen islands in the river. Shown here is one at Cap Tourmente National Wildlife Area. Oiled birds brought to centers are cleaned and checked by a veterinarian. They are fed and kept warm as they recuperate, and then they are released back into the wilderness.

Vacationing along the St. Lawrence offers a welcome escape for urban dwellers. Unfortunately, as more people come, changes to the water quality may result.

It is along the St. Lawrence River and the Great Lakes that agriculture and urban growth have peaked in Canada. Wetlands have been filled in for development to meet the growing needs for housing and business. Others have been drained for cropland and grazing land.

## Human Health Effects

Humans are threatened, as well. Toxins that get into the river and seaway are often eaten by small, bottom-dwelling organisms. Larger animals then eat the organisms, and the toxins are carried on up the food chain, becoming concentrated along the way, and eventually reaching humans.

When shellfish and wildlife contain high accumulations of toxins, the dangers for humans who eat them can be serious. A study of mothers who ate Lake Michigan fish poisoned with PCBs—chemicals that don't break down—showed that PCBs were passed to their children both in the womb and through breast milk. Babies were born smaller than normal, and many had coordination problems. In later years, these children grew slowly and had poor short-term memory.

People living in the region depended on fish as a major source of protein. But PCBs in the fish caused digestive problems and possibly cancer. Now unable to eat the fish, residents are forced to rely on less nutritious foods.

And what of our need for pure water? The Great Lakes hold 20 percent of the world's fresh surface water. Nearly 40 million people rely on the lakes for their drinking water every day. It becomes increasingly more costly and much more difficult to filter the impurities out of the water. Many residents near the Great Lakes and St. Lawrence have begun to drink bottled water.

## Introduced Species

In addition to pollution, big ships can also carry other invaders as well—marine plants and animals that did not originally inhabit the waters of the Great Lakes and the St. Lawrence River. More than 300 species of plants and animals that are not native to the Great Lakes have entered the lake waters since the opening of the seaway.

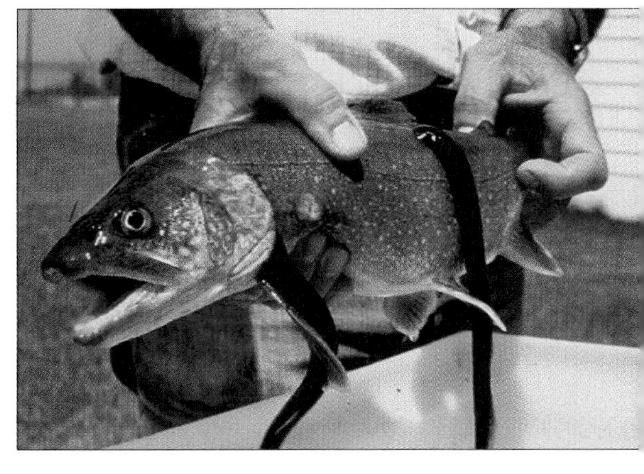

Sea lampreys hang on to their prey for several days as they suck out fluid and muscle tissues.

Some species thrive in the new environment, where, because they are not native inhabitants, they have no natural enemies. They become pests as they grow and reproduce, upsetting the delicate ecological balance of native plants and animals.

Alewives are such introduced pests. This fish, a member of the herring family, entered the Great Lakes from the Atlantic Ocean through the seaway and the Welland Canal. They multiplied so rapidly in the 1960s that they became a great nuisance. They have little commercial value, and they threaten the important native fish by competing for the same food source. In addition, they cost a great deal of money in cleanup operations because they periodically die by the millions, wash up on shores and beaches, and rot. Coho and chinook salmon were introduced to control these pests.

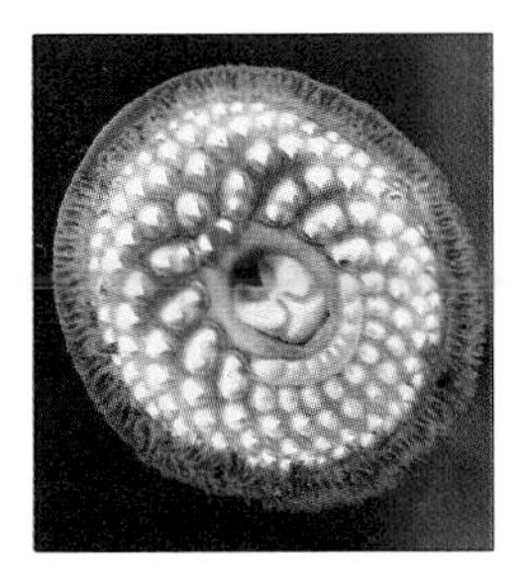

The sea lamprey attaches itself to fish with rows of sharp teeth that act like a suction cup.

The round, sucking mouths of sea lampreys are filled with horny teeth that latch onto their prey, mostly game fish. These parasitic fish, eellike and scaleless, range from about 6 to 40 inches (15 cm to 1 m) long. Though native to the coastal areas of the Atlantic Ocean, they entered the Great Lakes by way of the shipping channels of the St. Lawrence.

Their killing effects in the 1950s were disastrous—they nearly wiped out lake trout and other commercially valuable fish. Their population was finally brought under control by poisoning their breeding areas with a chemical that attacks the larvae.

These nesting structures on Île Blanche, Québec, were constructed by Ducks Unlimited Canada to provide a breeding place for waterfowl since many of the river's natural wetlands are gone.

## The Bottom Line

In looking at the Seaway System and its impact on the region, many effects, both good and bad, can be seen. The debate about whether it should have been built lingers on, especially when two questions are asked: Has the St. Lawrence Seaway paid off its debts? And has it fulfilled its early promise? Unfortunately, the answer to both questions is "no."

Money is still an issue. The Canadian government has had to increase its tolls at the locks to cover losses. The United States, which operates a smaller portion of the seaway, has not had as great a loss. Many people think that improved transportation and more jobs have not made up for the cost.

In the mid-1970s, seaway authorities predicted that the full capacity of the St. Lawrence Seaway would be realized by 1990. They were wrong about this, also.

In its first years of operation, the seaway transported about 30 million tons of cargo each year. This amount increased steadily, reaching a peak of 74 million tons in 1979. Since then, however, the transportation of cargo has declined. Today, the seaway transports less than 45 million tons per year, or approximately seven percent of the world's total. This is only half of what the seaway system could potentially carry.

This decline has been caused, in part, by such changes as the development of air freight and the shift of growing some crops in the West. Also, many freighters favored by today's shipping companies require a deeper, 37-foot (11-m) draft—too large to go through the locks. Enlarging the seaway would be very expensive. Once again, Canada and the United States are searching for answers to the problems of the St. Lawrence River and its Seaway System.

# Chapter Six

# Toward the Future

It's January, and winter has its icy claws clutched tightly around the cold northern reaches of the St. Lawrence River. Brilliant white snow is piled high among trees on the riverbanks, while eagles overhead survey the shimmering scene. Ice glistens on the surface, while below, in deeper, darker parts of the river, water still flows, and marine plants and animals move at a slow pace.

But into this tranquil environment comes something new on the winter scene. A massive ship, with a sharp, sturdy bow, pushes forward through the frozen water, breaking the ice before it, sending shards flying to the sides as it cuts a path toward an inland port. Waves rock the shoreline, smashing ice chunks into the banks.

The calm underwater scene is quickly transformed, as the ship's engines churn the water into a frenzy. Noise drives the shoreline birds and animals from their resting places, and they rush for cover from the fury. And then, as quickly as it moved into the picture, the ship is gone, leaving behind only the sound of rippling water and ice chunks settling back into position.

*"Despite the significance of the Great Lakes and our collective rhetoric to restore and enhance them, we as a society continue to mortgage our future by poisoning, suffocating, and otherwise threatening them because of insufficient knowledge, other priorities, and short-sightedness.*

*"What our generation has failed to realize is that, what we are doing to the Great Lakes, we are doing to ourselves and to our children."*

**— The International Joint Commission; *Fifth Biennial Report on Great Lakes Water Quality*, 1990**

## Winter Wonderland

Winter shipping on the St. Lawrence Seaway System—moving cargo and earning money there year-round—is still only a fantasy. There have been a few experiments with winter navigation in decades past, but the concept has not been seriously proposed for years—even though it's probably one of the least expensive ways to increase use of the seaway.

A light pillar near Île Blanche, Québec

Winter shipping would allow cargo to move twelve months of the year rather than the nine months or so that ships travel on the seaway now. It's possible that about 25 percent more cargo—about 10 million tons—would be transported. The ports could remain open year-round,

A Canadian Coast Guard ship breaks river ice during the spring season in order to prevent ice jams and flooding.

people would retain their jobs, and more money could be generated.

Of course, making the seaway navigable through the icy winter months would not be cheap. Only Lake Erie freezes completely, but the shorelines of all the Great Lakes freeze for several miles out, preventing entrance to the ports—and many locks and channels freeze shut as well. Icebreaker boats can plow through ice, of course, but the broken chunks of ice could jam the locks and block the water's entry to the power generators. Special structures would have to be built to prevent this problem.

Nevertheless, all this work would be less expensive than enlarging the seaway to handle bigger ships. Winter navigation was a rather popular idea in the 1970s, but opposition from various groups brought it to a halt.

First, the railroads fought it. They stood to lose a good deal of the cargo that they moved during the winter months when the seaway was out of operation. Even some of the port and shipowners were opposed—they felt they needed the downtime during winter to make necessary repairs.

But mostly, winter navigation was fought by environmentalists. It was the first real effort by environmental groups along the St. Lawrence River to unite for a major cause, and their voices were heard. A group named Save the River that was formed in upstate New York is still active today, both in the United States and Canada, monitoring activities on the St. Lawrence River.

Other opposition came from the New York State Department of Environmental Conservation, the U.S. Fish and Wildlife Service, and seamen's unions in Canada. These groups identified several types of environmental damage that would be caused by winter navigation.

Opponents to winter navigation on the St. Lawrence often point to increased erosion caused by waves and ice breaking off from the shoreline.

First, the delicate bottom ecology of the river, minute plants and animals, would be disturbed by the physical movements of ships. This movement is somewhat different in the winter than in summer, since the wave action in winter, when ice covers part of the river, follows a different pattern. There is great energy in waves under the ice. This energy has a tearing effect on the vegetation and soil structure of the riverbanks, as well as churning up the bottom. It rips shoreline ice from the land, taking fragile vegetation and nutrient-rich topsoil along with it.

Winter ecology would also be disturbed. For example, the eagles that winter in the seaway region depend upon open water areas for some of their food supply. The movement of the water in the river's channel keeps these areas open. In winter, big commercial ships would disturb and shift the frozen ice cover, destroying these feeding areas.

Small boats were allowed to travel on the badly polluted Lachine Canal until 1981. Commerical traffic stopped in 1970. The best method for cleaning the contaminated canal has not been identified yet.

Ships traveling through the river and seaway would break up the ice cover, possibly causing serious winter flooding. And winter navigation would also increase the number of accidents, particularly with single-hulled oil tankers. It would be difficult to clean up an oil spill during winter, since weather conditions are often harsh.

"We were clobbered by environmentalists," said Robert Lewis of the St. Lawrence Seaway Development Corporation, recalling his office's push for winter navigation.

## Environmentalists to the Fore

Victory over winter navigation gave encouragement to other environmental groups with interests along the St. Lawrence River. More organizations have formed, and thousands of people have joined the crusade to preserve what remains of the natural life along the river and seaway. Local, state, provincial, and federal governments have rallied for environmental causes, and laws protecting nature have been enacted.

Shipping interests will obviously continue to dominate the St. Lawrence River. But it is likely that environmental groups, working with the shipping industry, will do much to shape the future, as programs protecting nature gather steam.

For example, one of the main ways of attacking pollution in the St. Lawrence previously had been to regulate and fine polluters. This method was only partially successful, however, because it took effect only after the damage had been done. Now, the major emphasis—in the courts, in business, and in grassroots efforts—is on prevention of pollution. Today, there are tight restrictions on the use, production, and discharge of pollutants.

Gannets nesting on Île Bonaventure, Québec

## Preventing Pollution

This prevention of pollution can be seen clearly in the United States Oil Pollution Act of 1990. One measure taken by the shipping industry in response is a new requirement for double-hulled tank vessels, which are much less likely to leak their contents in an accident. The complete phase-out of all single-hulled vessels will begin in 1995 and is expected to take 20 years.

The Great Lakes/St. Lawrence Pollution Prevention Initiative, a $25-million program begun in March 1991, is working to stop pollution before it starts. This U.S.-Canadian program is dedicated to involving all of society in reducing toxic pollutants.

Participating in the program are automotive-manufacturing plants and plants that manufacture automotive parts, generators of small quantities of hazardous wastes, and local communities. They all work to reduce the amount of pollutants entering the St. Lawrence. The Pollution Prevention Centre, headquartered in Sarnia, Ontario, has the responsibility for increasing awareness of the program's work and of pollution prevention throughout the region.

Beautiful Mingan Archipelago is located in a Zone of Prime Concern.

A similar effort taking place in Canada alone involves various regions called the Zones of Prime Concern. These zones—23 of them—have been identified along the St. Lawrence River. Within these specific regions, plans are being made on the local level to prevent an increase in pollution. Residents are involved, along with local governments, businesses, and industries.

To make these efforts effective, attitudes need to change, too. People living along the river, as well as people who use it, managers of local industry, and leaders of local government all need to understand the importance of the St. Lawrence. Many other conservation and environmental groups are working to educate people about the river in order to protect its future.

## Saving the Land

The Thousand Islands Land Trust (TILT) is an American nonprofit organization determined to preserve the beauty and natural resources of the Thousand Islands region. More than 3,000 acres (1,214 ha) of property in the area have been protected by TILT. In addition, the group works to protect wetlands and other habitats of the region's threatened or endangered species and fisheries. It supports the purchase of recreation areas for public use and funds various environmental research projects.

Different organizations, such as the Thousand Islands Land Trust, are working to preserve the natural resources and beauty of the Thousand Islands region.

Most all of the land preservation by TILT is accomplished through agreements with private landowners called conservation easements. Nearly any parcel of land with specific environmental value can be preserved in this way, be it a forest, wetland, farm, or beach. The owners agree to preserve the land following specific guidelines, and this agreement accompanies the land even after it is sold—new owners are legally bound to follow the restrictions. In return, owners are eligible for reductions in taxes, and they have the satisfaction of knowing they have done something to retain their land's natural beauty forever.

In addition to the Thousand Islands region, the Lachine Canal has also received a great deal of attention. Since 1981, this canal had been off-limits to public recreational boat traffic because it was dangerously polluted. However, plans are being made to clean and reopen the canal in the future.

Researchers are looking at ways to make this section of the seaway a great place to visit once again. But because it is located in a heavily populated area, the social, legal, and economic aspects of the cleanup must be considered along with the scientific methods. In particular, contaminated sediments must be removed and stored safely in a way that is not unsightly.

## Sediment Solutions

Dealing with contaminated sediments that are dredged out of the canals and waterways has posed problems in many areas along the seaway. Various techniques for dealing with the waste are being tested. Rather than simply dumping the sediment into landfills, the dredged material may be used to construct artificial islands or new wildlife habitats.

Researchers in Toledo, Ohio, are studying what is being called an "ultimate recycling contained disposal facility." Slightly contaminated sludge from the Toledo port's shipping channels is dried and mixed with yard waste, such as grass clippings and leaves, lime, and sewage treatment sludge, to create a topsoil that is safe and usable. If it works, such composting will be tried along the seaway as a long-term solution to the problem of sludge disposal.

The peregrine falcon is making a comeback in Canada and the United States as polluted waters are cleaned up.

## The Action Plan

Perhaps the largest and most unified effort at saving the environment of the St. Lawrence is the St. Lawrence Action Plan, launched in June 1988 by the government of Canada.

The Action Plan's goals include the following:

- 90 percent reduction in the amount of liquid toxic waste that 50 targeted industrial plants were dumping into the St. Lawrence River,
- restoration of wetlands and contaminated federal sites in the region,
- development of a marine park at the mouth of the Saguenay River in order to protect 12,350 acres (5,000 ha) of nearby wildlife habitat, and
- recovery of endangered species.

These goals are being implemented by an organization called the St. Lawrence Centre, created by a group of scientists.

The development of beach property along the north shore of the St. Lawrence has destroyed a habitat of the endangered piping plover.

In dealing with liquid toxic wastes in the river, the center is working with industry to develop new ways to control and reduce the amount of waste being dumped. Nearly 30 stations have been set up to study the impact of chemicals in the water and to research ways of dealing with them.

Many of the 50 industries targeted to reduce toxic waste do not discharge toxins directly into the river. Instead, they contaminate the air and surrounding land with pollutants. Chemicals in the air often settle into the water. Chemicals in the land leach (mix with rainwater and run down) into the groundwater and eventually flow into the river. New methods to reduce these pollutants are being sought. For example, Cascades, Inc., which manufactures tar paper, has acquired a special machine that treats gas emissions to make them safer.

To protect endangered species, a team representing both the federal government and the province has prepared a list of vulnerable species—animals

Waterfowl such as this blue-winged teal depend on habitat along the river's shoreline to live and breed.

and plants that are endangered and facing probable extinction—living in the St. Lawrence River and surrounding waterways. Various projects to preserve these species are under way.

## Saguenay Marine Park

The beluga whales that live in the St. Lawrence River near the mouth of the Saguenay River have received special attention. Thousands of these unusual mammals once swam in these waters, but only a few hundred remain today. Many were killed by a brutal hunting industry, which was finally outlawed in 1980. But now the belugas have fallen victim to the pollutants that contaminate their habitat. Both the St. Lawrence and the Saguenay rivers contain large amounts of toxins that threaten the belugas as well as their food sources.

An aerial count of the beluga population has been made, and their food sources were studied for contamination. In addition, the carcasses of several belugas—found dead and washed ashore—were analyzed to determine the causes of death.

The chemical contaminants have produced a variety of ill effects in the belugas, such as premature births and other reproduction difficulties. Other problems include bladder cancer and viral diseases that aren't normally found in belugas, which suggests that the pollution decreases the animals' immunity to disease.

The Saguenay Marine Park was created in an effort to save the beluga whales, as well as many other species that live in the St. Lawrence River. Located at the confluence of the St. Lawrence and the Saguenay rivers, the park was established in 1990 to help preserve the environment and its abundance of unusual wildlife.

Several species are already gone, including the walruses that once thrived at the mouth of the Saguenay. European hunters on the St. Lawrence killed these massive sea mammals for the oil that could be taken from their blubber, their ivory tusks, and their heavy hides. Most were gone by the year 1800. Today, there is a determined effort to save the animals that remain, including the unique species of whales that have lived there for centuries.

The park is located in the region that bears the greatest amount of pollution in Canada, caused by the industrial growth along the St. Lawrence River, as well as agriculture and forestry along both rivers. Although these sources of pollution are outside the marine park's boundaries, the contaminants still flow into the park. The marine park designation will

**Thousands of tourists flock to the banks of the St. Lawrence to watch the protected whales. The contamination from industrial growth, agriculture, and forestry along the river will be closely monitored to keep the whales safe.**

help to improve water quality as pollutants are monitored more closely, and the work of those fighting to stop contamination is supported.

Other actions within the park include the development of survival plans for its endangered species, restoration of wetlands, and protection of the habitat of many park animals. A large variety of plants and animals make their homes here—from large marine mammals and amazing varieties of fish to unusual types of algae.

**The future of the St. Lawrence Seaway, the river's natural ecology, and the economic prospects of the entire region are tied together. All interests must work together to keep the river healthy.**

## Making up for the Past

The Great Lakes-St. Lawrence Seaway System and the St. Lawrence River have been vital parts of North American history and the growth of its economy. The natural world on which it is based is truly one of the wonders of the world. The work of the future calls for bringing together those two different aspects of the waterway. Though much has been accomplished, much more remains to be done.

Michel P. Lamontagne, the executive director of the St. Lawrence Centre, wrote in 1992: "The progress achieved so far has been remarkable. Scientific research has had very practical results . . . (But) the battle for the river is not over yet. These years of hard work have not been enough to compensate for a century of negligence."

## GLOSSARY

**canal** – an artificial or improved waterway connecting two bodies of water and used for shipping and other water transportation.

**commodity** – an article or product that is transported for trade.

**contamination** – a process of making a material impure by adding another material.

**dredging** – digging mud and sludge off a river bottom to increase the depth of the water.

**generator** – a device that produces electricity by changing mechanical energy (from motion) into electrical energy. The motion of a coil of copper wire within a magnetic field produces the electron flow—electricity—within a wire. A turbine in an electric power plant produces the mechanical motion for the generator.

**groundwater** – water that flows beneath the Earth's surface. The level of the groundwater determines the level of a river or lake.

**hazardous waste** – a discarded chemical capable of harming the environment or causing illness or death to living things.

**hydroelectric power** – electric power produced by using the force of moving water to turn turbines.

**lock** – a section of waterway, closed off by gates at both ends, in which the water level can be changed to allow vessels to be raised and lowered. Locks allow a ship to travel beyond a waterfall or other obstacle in the waterway.

**petroleum** – a thick, flammable chemical found beneath the Earth's surface, typically processed into gasoline, kerosene, oils, asphalt, and a variety of other products.

**pollutant** – any material that is harmful to living organisms, air, or water, when it is released into the environment.

**runoff** – rainwater that flows off land into waterways, often carrying chemicals used in agriculture and petroleum products from highways.

**sediment** – any material, previously suspended in water, that settles onto a surface.

**sludge** – sediment or solid material that settles out of water and sinks to the bottom.

**toxin** – a chemical that is poisonous and harmful to people and other organisms.

**turbine** – a rotating device that is turned by the pressure of air or liquid against its blades. In a hydroelectric power plant, the turbines are turned by the force of falling water.

**wetlands** – low-lying land areas that flood all or part of the year, such as marshes and swamps.

## FOR MORE INFORMATION


Chevrier, Lionel. *The St. Lawrence Seaway.* Toronto: Macmillan, 1959.
Emmond, Kenneth D. *Québec.* Chicago: Childrens Press, 1992.
Judson, Clara Ingram. *St. Lawrence Seaway.* Chicago: Follett, 1959.
LeVert, Suzanne. *Québec.* New York/Philadelphia: Chelsea House, 1991.
Mabee, Carleton. *The Seaway Story.* New York: Macmillan, 1961.
MacLennan, Hugh. *Rivers of Canada.* Toronto: Macmillan, 1974.
Malcolm, Andrew H. *The Land and People of Canada.* New York: HarperCollins, 1991.
Mason, Philip. *The Scenic St. Lawrence.* Niagara Falls, Ontario: Travelpic, 1968.
*Science Leading to Action: The St. Lawrence.* The St. Lawrence Centre, Environment Canada. Montréal, Québec: Published by the Authority of the Minister of the Environment. Minister of Supply and Services, Canada, 1991.
Sunday, Jane M. *Canada.* Austin, TX: Raintree Steck-Vaughn, 1993.
*Water for Life,* Greenpeace, 1989.
Wortik, Nancy. *The French Canadians.* New York/Philadelphia: Chelsea House, 1989.

# INDEX